STARTUP GUIDE

#startupeverywhere

Startup Guide Stockholm V.2

EDITORIAL
Publisher: Sissel Hansen
Editor: Marissa van Uden
Proofreader: Michelle Mills
Contributing Editor: Charmaine Li
Staff Writers: Alex Gerald, Charmaine Li, John Sperryn, L. Isaac Simon,
Jesse Van Mouwerik, Alexandra Connerty, Shelley Pascual
Contributing Writers: Matthew Speiser, Phineas Rueckert, Nadine Freischlad,
Hedda Langeby, Michelle Arrouas, Cara Eisenpress, Maria Cometto

PRODUCTION
Head of Production: Tim Rhodes
Researchers: Morgane Oléron, Sonia Kaurah, Hedda Langeby

DESIGN & PHOTOGRAPHY
Designer: Ines Pedro
Photographers: Christopher Backholm

Additional photography by Unsplash.com, Mercedes-Benz,
Crelle Photography, Elisabeth Ingvar, SAS

Illustrations by Joana Carvalho
Photo Editor: Daniela Carducci

SALES & DISTRIBUTION
Head of Sales: Marlene do Vale marlene@startupguide.com
Head of Community Growth: Eglė Duleckytė egle@startupguide.com
Head of Business Development: Anna Weissensteiner anna@startupguide.com
Head of Distribution: İrem Topçuoğlu irem@startupguide.com

Printed in Berlin, Germany by
Medialis-Offsetdruck GmbH
Heidelbergerstraße 65, 12435 Berlin

Published by Startup Guide World IVS
Kanonbådsvej 2, 1437 Copenhagen K

info@startupguide.com
Visit us: startupguide.com
@StartupGuideHQ

Worldwide distribution by Die Gestalten
Visit: gestalten.com

ISBN: 978-3-947624-04-1

STARTUP GUIDE STOCKHOLM

volume 2

STARTUP GUIDE STOCKHOLM

In partnership with **SUP46**

Proudly supported by

Sissel Hansen
/ Startup Guide

Many consider Stockholm one of the leading startup capitals in the Nordics – and one of the top in the world. Some even call it a "second Silicon Valley." It's no surprise, considering Stockholm was the birthplace of companies such as Skype, Klarna, King (maker of Candy Crush) and Mojang (creator of Minecraft) all went from small startups to billion-dollar juggernauts. Music streaming giant Spotify is also headquartered in the Swedish capital. According to a study by investment firm Atomico in 2015, the city has the second highest number of unicorns per capita in the world, with 6.3 billion-dollar companies per million people (behind Silicon Valley with 8.1). Perhaps the city's small population has pushed startups to look beyond its borders and consider a global approach from day one.

In the last decade, Stockholm's startup scene has risen through the ranks to become a hotbed for innovation, especially when it comes to the fields of gaming, music streaming and fintech. Some huge contributing factors to the ecosystem's incredible growth include the city's high concentration of programmers and the immense governmental support offered to startups, as well as the non-hierarchical nature of Swedish leadership. It doesn't hurt that Sweden has one of the most advanced digital economies in the EU and is one of the most gender-equal countries in the world. From 2007 to 2014, the Swedish Government ran a program to further promote women's entrepreneurship during the period. The Swedes also take work-life balance very seriously – as in, the concept actually exists here and isn't only a myth like in some other startup hubs around the world.

Stockholm's unicorns have brought the city a lot of international attention and attracted a new wave of talent. Since our last edition in 2016, its startup ecosystem has become even more mature and connected, so it's the perfect time for us to uncover new insights, trends and entrepreneur stories for Startup Guide Stockholm Vol. 2. We can't wait for you to be immersed in the city's startup community once again.

Sissel Hansen
Founder and CEO of Startup Guide

Local Community Partner / SUP46

Entrepreneurship and risk-taking behavior is in the air in Stockholm, and if you stay long enough, you'll soon feel it too. A determination to build the best products, a passion for tech, and incredible focus combined with modesty are all traits anchored in the Swedish culture and traditions. This makes the Swedish capital a wonderful place to start pursuing your dreams and to turn your ideas into a reality.

Swedes have always been early adopters, and great Swedish success stories such as Spotify, iZettle, Klarna, Mojang, King and Skype are no coincidences. In the early '80s, Sweden was one of the first countries in Europe with internet access; in the '90s, the government subsidized PCs for private households, resulting in almost everyone growing up with a computer and an internet connection. Early adoption is just one of many factors that have given Swedes a serious competitive advantage.

Sweden already had a world-renowned tech scene, but it was missing a platform to help entrepreneurs connect with the support they need to succeed even faster. This is why three pioneers started SUP46 (Start-Up People of Sweden) in 2013 in the heart of Stockholm. They shared a common vision: to create a tech paradise for entrepreneurs and put Swedish startups on the map.

Five years later, SUP46 is the number-one hub for the Swedish startup scene, providing selected companies with an environment that nurtures passion, innovation and growth. We work together to help our members become global game-changers. We offer a wide range of support to help our startups scale, including but not limited to connecting the community, matchmaking with investors and providing PR, recruitment and support for international expansion. SUP46 also works with relevant partners, has a Startup Cafe with an open work space, and hosts over two hundred events and workshops a year.

We believe in the power of the community and are convinced that together the possibilities are endless. This is why we will continue working hand in hand with great partners such as *The Startup Guide*.

It's our mission to make Stockholm an even better place for entrepreneurs, where unicorns are not a rare breed anymore.

Morgane Oléron (Project Coordinator)   Sonia Kaurah (Community Manager)

contents

STARTUP
GUIDE
STOCKHOLM

startups

spaces

programs

experts

founders

Local Ecosystem

[Facts & Figures]
- With numerous well-known research institutes, such as the Royal Institute of Technology (KTH), Karolinska Institutet (KI), Stockholm University (SU), Södertörn University and Stockholm School of Economics, conditions for innovation in Stockholm are excellent.
- 62.1% of people aged between 30 and 34 are educated to a tertiary level – notably higher than the national average of 51% and substantially higher than the EU's average of 39.1%.
- The high-tech sector in Stockholm employs 95,000 people, representing just over 40% of people employed in this sector across all of Sweden and nearly 8% of Sweden's total employment.
- The Milken Institute's inaugural Best-Performing Cities Europe index rated Stockholm as the second-best performing city in Europe.
- Sweden has the second-largest concentration of billion-dollar companies per capita in the world (with 6.3 billion-dollar companies per million people, trailing only Silicon Valley at 8.1).
- In 2016, a record 38 tech companies pulled in more than 1.5 billion SEK (approximately US$160 million) in capital through IPOs.

[Notable Startups]
- Spotify, valued at US$8.5 billion in 2011, has now launched on the New York Stock Exchange with a value of US$29.5 billion (as of April 2018).
- King Digital, maker of Candy Crush, was bought by Activision Blizzard for US$5.9 billion in 2016.

Sources: ec.europa.eu, forbes.com, investstockholm.com, milkeninstitute.org, atomico.com/explore-d3, nordic.businessinsider.com, techcrunch.com

[City] # Stockholm, Sweden

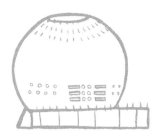

[Statistics:]
Urban population: **1.54 million**
Metropolitan population: **2.32 million**
Area: **381.6 km²**
GDP: **US$166,785 (million)**

STARTUP GUIDE STOCKHOLM

Intro to the City

Stockholm is a beautiful, trendy and forward-looking city with a strong collective interest in the new and the possible. So maybe it's not surprising that the city sits high in global startup rankings and attracts innovative people from all around the world. Stockholm is the home of companies such as Skype, Candy King, Spotify and Mojang and has been named the world's second-leading startup ecosystem after Silicon Valley by investment firm Sparklabs. Although forward-looking, history has a strong presence in the city, which was founded in 1252. This is seen in the architecture across the city's fourteen islands, from the narrow cobbled streets and colorful houses in Gamla stan (the Old Town) to the old wooden houses and alleys of Södermalm, both of which transport you back centuries. There are also the luxurious stone-and-brick buildings from the turn of the last century on the exclusive esplanade Strandvägen on Östermalm.

Stockholmers are early adopters when it comes to technology, fashion, food and culture, but they also enjoy their traditions, such as leaving the city for the countryside or for the archipelago to celebrate Midsummer in late June, or queueing up for Allsång på Skansen, the annual singalong concerts held during the summer in the city's open-air museum Skansen. It is perhaps the balance between the old and the new – the tried and tested and the innovative – that is a defining characteristic of the city and its inhabitants.

Before You Come

Swedes are impressed by any foreigner who makes the effort to learn the language.
Don't worry about not speaking Swedish when you first arrive – you'll easily get by with English
– but it won't hurt to learn some key vocabulary such as "*Hej!*" ("Hi") and "*tack så mycket*"
("thank you very much").

If you're moving to Stockholm as an EU or EEA citizen, you can stay for up to three months
without any requirements; but if you're planning to stay longer, you must either have
employment, be self-employed or be able to prove that you have sufficient funds to support
yourself (including paying for health insurance). If you're a citizen of a non-EU or non-EEA
country, a visa is required for stays up to ninety days. If you plan to stay longer, start a business
or run a business, you must apply for a residence permit, and this must be ready before you
arrive in Stockholm. For further information, visit the Swedish Migration Agency
(Migrationsverket) website (**www.migrationsverket.se**).

Cost of Living

Stockholm is not known as a cheap city to live in, but there are certainly things you can do
to make living more affordable. Public transport in Stockholm is a great way to get around
the city, but biking is a cheaper option and the city is well served with bike lanes. The biggest
expense in the city is housing. In terms of housing costs, a general rule of thumb (perhaps
not surprising) is that the further away from the city center you go, the cheaper housing is.

Food can be costly, and although Stockholm offers a great range of restaurants, bars and cafés,
cooking at home is a sure way to keep your spending down. There are budget grocery chains
such as Lidl and Willys across the city, and further out in the suburbs you'll find chains such
as Ica Maxi that can help you keep food spending down. You can also take after many locals
and bring a home-cooked meal for your work lunch.

Cultural Differences

Stockholm and Sweden are characterized by a high degree of social trust, which translates into a strong belief that most people will do the right thing and act responsibly. This high degree of trust also extends to the government, and Swedes therefore have no qualms about their *personnummer* (personal identity number) being used by the government authorities and agencies in all matter of situations. In Sweden, gender equality is also very important. This is reflected in men and women being equally active on the labor market, and it's not an unusual sight to see fathers pushing strollers. When you arrive in Stockholm, you'll notice a lot of queueing, whether at the bus stop, at the alcohol retailer Systembolaget, or at the tax office. Either a queue forms naturally or you must take a number at a queue machine. Either way, you can be sure that you'll be queueing.

Renting an Apartment

When renting, landlords are sure to ask for your ID, references and proof of employment, so have all your documents ready. Finding a rental apartment in Stockholm can be time consuming, as demand is high and landlords can afford to be picky about who they rent to. The rental contracts are usually for six months up to one year. After one year, the apartment owner is usually required to apply to his or her housing cooperative for approval to sublet for another year. If approved, you could get a one-year extension.

There are many websites to visit when searching for a rental apartment. The most popular ones include www.blocket.se and www.bostaddirekt.com. In both cases, you can also post your own profile with references and information about what you're looking for. This makes you searchable by landlords and can be an efficient way of finding an apartment. There are also Facebook groups you can join, such as the "Looking for Accommodation in Stockholm?" group or "Rooms/Housing Stockholm."

See **Flats and Rentals** page **189**

Finding a Coworking Space

As the startup scene in Stockholm has grown in recent years, so has the range of coworking spaces. They offer various membership options and are available in many central and well-connected locations across the city, including the Vasastan, Norrmalm and Östermalm boroughs. The spaces offer a range of amenities and range from classic office buildings to modernized industrial buildings and even the grand hall of an old tram station. Many coworking spaces specialize in certain industries, such as H2 Health Hub, which is geared towards health-tech innovators, entrepreneurs and startups; Norrsken House, with its focus on impact entrepreneurs; or STHLM Music City, for music creators, music tech innovators and industry professionals. Some of Stockholm's coworking spaces cater to not only your working needs but also your well-being and social life, offering regular after-works (like startup hub SUP46 and The Park do) or weekly meditation and yoga (as offered by A house).

See **Spaces** page **72**

Insurance

In order to be covered by Swedish public health insurance, you must register with the Swedish Population Register. You do this via Skatteverket, the Swedish Tax Agency, which will give you your personnummer. Once you've been registered, you're entitled to public healthcare. Ultimately, Försäkringskassan (the Swedish Social Insurance Agency) determines whether or not you are insured in Sweden. Typically, if you work in Sweden, you're also generally insured in Sweden. This means you can also be entitled to different compensation schemes via Försäkringskassan. Some benefits are resident-based and others work-based. To be certain about what applies to your specific case, consult the Swedish Tax Agency's website, www.skatteverket.se.

If you're an EU, EEA or Swiss citizen and you're planning to stay in Stockholm for a shorter period of time, you need only pay the standard patient fee and show your European Health Insurance Card to receive necessary healthcare. If you're a citizen of a country outside the EU, EEA or Switzerland, generally you must pay the full cost of your healthcare yourself.

See **Insurance Companies** page **190**

Visas and Work Permits

EU/EEA citizens are free to live and work in Stockholm without a residence permit. You have the right of residence if you're employed, self-employed or starting a business, or if you can prove that you have sufficient means to support yourself. If you're a family member of an EU citizen with the right of residence, you also have the right of residence. If you're a Swiss citizen, you're also free to live and work in Stockholm, but you must apply for a residence permit. You can, however, start working before your application is processed. In all cases you must still register for your personnummer from Skatteverket. If you're a citizen of a non-EU country, you must have a job offer to apply for a work permit before entering Sweden. It is your Swedish employer that initiates your application by making an offer of employment via Migrationsverket (the Swedish Migration Agency).

See **Important Government Offices** page **190**

Taxes

As an employee in Sweden, municipal income tax will be withdrawn from your gross salary every month before it's paid out to you by your employer. Depending on your income bracket, you may also be subject to state income tax. You'll also be assigned a skattekonto, a tax account where all your tax payments will be shown, including your preliminary tax and your final tax notice. Every year, by 15 April, you'll receive your tax return from Skatteverket, which you must file. Submitting your tax return can be done in several ways, such as by text message, phone, app, e-service or on paper. You can find detailed information in English about filing your tax return on Skatteverket's website, www.skatteverket.se. When filing your return for the first time, it may be a good idea to contact Skatteverket to make sure that you understand the process fully.

See **Accountants** page **189**

Starting a Company

Starting a business in Sweden can be a fairly simple process. Once you have your business idea and plan, you should register your business with Bolagsverket, the Swedish Companies Registrations Office. You can register your business as *enskild näringsidkare* (sole trader), a limited liability company, a trading partnership, limited partnership or economic association. You then apply for approval for F-skatt (F-tax) and register with Skatteverket. Depending on what kind of business you have, you may also have to register for *moms* (VAT). You can find more information about this in English on Skatteverket's website.

There is a lot of support available for entrepreneurs in Sweden, and you can turn to advisory services such as Almi, IFS (the International Entrepreneurs Association in Sweden), the Stockholm Chamber of Commerce and NyföretagarCentrum for advice and help with everything from planning to securing financing.

See **Programs** page **52**

Opening a Bank Account

To open a bank account in Sweden, you'll need to meet with a bank advisor and bring some proof of identity such as an EU-card or passport. The bank may also ask for an identification letter from your bank in your home country. For a standard service package including a Visa or Mastercard, a private account, and internet- and telephone-banking services, you can expect to pay between 240–470 SEK per year. Some banks may also include pension advice in such a package. Popular banks in Sweden include Danske Bank (see page 128) , Nordea, Handelsbanken, Swedbank and SEB.

Stockholm is practically a cash-free city, and you can count on being able to use your credit card more or less everywhere. In fact, there are plenty of businesses, ranging from public buses to bars, that don't even accept cash. Swish is a popular mobile-payment app used to make smaller money transfers and payments and often used among friends or by small businesses.

See **Banks** page **189**

Getting Around

Stockholm has an excellent public transport system run by Storstockholms Lokaltrafik (SL). This includes subway, buses, tramlines, commuter trains and ferries covering the city center and suburbs, making it easy to get around safely and efficiently. To pay for travel, you can purchase either an SL Access card that you top up as you go, a ticket through SL's app, or a travel card for a fixed period. Biking is also a popular mode of transport in Stockholm, and you'll find a good network of bike lanes across the city. Locals bike all year around and are diligent helmet users. If you choose to bike in the winter, don't forget to switch to winter tires before the first snow! The same goes for car owners. Should you need a car just for a weekend or a short trip to IKEA, there are several carpooling services available, e.g., Sunfleet, Bilpoolen.nu, DriveNow and Move About. The latter offers electric cars only.

Phone and Internet

Tre, Telenor, Comviq, Telia and Tele2 are among the most popular mobile phone operators in Sweden, and they also offer internet services via mobile broadband. These companies usually offer fixed-rate deals that include free minutes and SMS/MMS, and then you pay for the mobile data you want in addition. It has become increasingly common for operators to offer contracts without any fixed contract time, but in some cases there can be contract periods of twelve to twenty-four months. This is often the case with special offers on the latest mobile phone models, so don't forget to ask the salesperson or read the fine print. Should you prefer a prepaid mobile-phone service, these are available via Hallon, Halebop and Lyca. You can either order sim cards via the operators' own websites or buy them in kiosks such as 7Eleven and Pressbyrån.

Learning the Language

Most Swedes are happy to speak English and do it well, so you won't have any trouble getting by in English, but if you really want to immerse yourself, learning Swedish doesn't hurt. Svenska för invandrare (SFI) is the municipally-organized language school for immigrants looking to learn Swedish and it is free of charge. Anyone who is over sixteen years old and living in Sweden, and who lacks basic knowledge in Swedish, is eligible for SFI. Folkuniversitetet, an adult educational association that provides SFI, also offers a more fast-paced program for people with higher education who may be looking to continue studying at university or getting a qualified job. There are also many digital tools you can use to learn Swedish, such as the Duolingo and UTalk apps. Once you've gotten the basics and want to practice conversation, you can also visit the language cafés offered by many local libraries.

See **Language Schools** page **190**

Meeting People

Swedes have a reputation for being a bit reserved, and maybe this is not entirely unwarranted, but if you're genuine and persistent when trying to meet and get to know people, you can certainly make very good friends. A good way to meet people is through work, where the *fika* (coffee break) that many workplaces have offers you a chance to chat with colleagues about non-work related things. Many workplaces and coworking spaces in Stockholm also organize *afterwork*, where colleagues meet in a casual setting for drinks and conversation after the workday. Facebook also offers many opportunities to get to know like-minded people in the city, bringing together expats and locals through shared hobbies and common interests. Examples include "Run with me Stockholm," "Expats World Stockholm" and "The International Club - Stockholm Expat Meetup Group."

See **Startup Events** page **190**

start

ups

[Name] # Airinum

[Elevator Pitch] *"Air pollution, bacteria and other airborne particles such as pollen impact our health and well-being. At Airinum, we empower individuals to breathe clean air by offering innovative products that intersect functionality and design, catering to urban citizens all over the world."*

[The Story] In the fall of 2014, Airinum cofounder Alexander Hjertstrom moved from Sweden to India. The people, scents and food of India created a life that was uniquely colorful, but something troubled him. Since moving, his long-gone asthma had started to come back. He realized he was becoming another victim of air pollution. After searching for a means to protect himself, Alex found that wearing an anti-pollution breathing mask was the most effective way. To his surprise, however, most of the masks on the market were very basic and far from perfect in their construction. Their designs were primitive, reminiscent of the masks worn by dentists or miners – not something you'd want to wear every day. When he returned to Sweden, Alexander discussed this problem with his old friends Fredrik, Johannes and Mehdi. Living in Sweden, clean air was something they all took for granted.

Realizing that not everyone can breathe clean and healthy Scandinavian air, they decided to do something about it, and Airinum was born. The company ran a successful Kickstarter campaign, raising over US$75,000, which validated their first attempt at creating and delivering their air-mask product. Further fine-tuning to the mask and filters have led to a second-generation product and limited editions. Much of their focus now is in expanding the distributor network, collaborating with major brands and raising awareness about air quality.

[Funding History]

Bootstrap   Seed   Angel

Airinum was initially bootstrapped. They then ran a successful Kickstarter campaign, which ran from December 2015 and into 2016 and raised US$75,000. Two Seed rounds were backed by Daniel Pilotti, founder of Ryska Posten, and the Angel network DHS Venture Partners.

[Milestones]
- Launching Sweden's most backed "fashion" Kickstarter project during 2015
- Shipping the first generation of products in 2016
- Launching the global web-shop along with online marketplaces in China such as Tmall and JD
- Expanding growth through offline distribution in more than ten countries and launching the second-generation product in 2018

[Links] Web: **airinum.com** Facebook: **airinum** Twitter: **@airinumab** Instagram: **airinum**

[Name]   # Amuse

[Elevator Pitch]   *"We're changing the music industry for the better. Artists of today want to be in control, so we rethought distribution, artist discovery and record deals. We're a record company that offers free music distribution to independent artists around the world."*

[The Story]   Amuse was founded in 2015 in Stockholm by Diego Farias and four cofounders, who were on a mission to shake up the music industry. The experienced team of tech- and music-industry veterans had seen firsthand the changes in the industry, and decided to rethink how new music should be distributed and discovered. They designed their free mobile-based Amuse app and brought it to market. The budding artist creates an account on the app and then submits their music and artwork for release. Once the release is approved, it's delivered to all major music services. The artist can then follow the streaming and download progress through the app and later withdraw royalties.

If Amuse discovers an artist it believes in, it will offer them a record deal that includes marketing, financing, promotion and playlist pitching. Amuse pays for the project but thereafter splits the profits 50/50 with the artist, and this business model enables them to make distribution free of charge. Amuse is passionate about wanting artists to own their music, and it only makes license deals in which the artist retains ownership their work, so that after the contract period is over the artist is free to do whatever they want with their music.

[Funding History]

Bootstrap   Seed   Angel   External

Amuse started by bootstrapping but by 2016 it had raised initial investment of approximately €285,000. It soon caught the imagination of music entrepreneur Will.i.am, who joined the team in summer 2017. This was followed by a €3.5 million A-round in August 2017 and another A-round in late Spring 2018.

[Milestones]
- Bringing in the first Angel investor in January 2016
- Completing the strong cofounding team by April 2016
- Completing the successful first A-round in 2017
- Celebrating the first platinum single in March 2018 under the Amuse record label

[Links]   Web: **amuse.io** Facebook: **amuse.io** Twitter: **@amuse_io** Instagram: **amuse.io**

[Name]

Gleechi

[Elevator Pitch]

"We develop software solutions to enable hand interaction between humans, computers and robots."

[The Story]

Gleechi is based on the work of Kai Hübner and Dan Song, two robotics researchers at the KTH Royal Institute of Technology in Stockholm who developed a predictive algorithm that analyzes the shape and orientation of an object and translates that into instructions for how it should be grasped. Initially, the code was applied to tell robots how to pick up physical things. It could steer five-fingered, human-like hands or robotic hands with just three fingers, and it worked with any type of object. The researchers soon realized their algorithm could also work in virtual environments and saw many possible commercial applications for their software, and so Gleechi was founded in 2014, with Jakob Johansson joining as CEO.

The startup's first major client was a game developer. Gleechi adapted its algorithm to help players have a more immersive and realistic experience when picking up items in-game. But now Johansson is taking Gleechi beyond gaming and finding ways to use its software in virtual training environments (for example, to teach workers how to handle dangerous machines) or in healthcare (for example, for rehabilitative exercises in virtual environments to help stroke patients). Gleechi's eight-person team is still creating custom-tailored solutions for its clients, but it's hoping to shift to a software-as-a-service model, where clients can log in and customize the software to suit their needs by themselves.

[Funding History]

Bootstrap   Seed

Gleechi received seed funding in September 2016 from ALMI Invest through the EIT Digital Accelerator in the form of convertible debt. The company has otherwise been bootstrapped and has been able to sustain itself with prize money from competitions and its paying customers.

[Milestones]
- Winning our first paying customer, a game developer
- Getting invited to speak at the biggest stage at the Game Developer Conference
- Realizing VR gaming is still an immature industry, and finding ways to apply our tech for learning and health
- Landing our first major commercial application for VR training

[Links] Web: **gleechi.com**

[Name]
Hi Henry

[Elevator Pitch]
"We're an employee-experience platform that enables companies to take better care of their employees from onboarding to exit. Our AI-powered office assistant, Hi Henry, is designed to make life at work easier and more productive."

[The Story]
After several years of helping businesses develop strategy and manage major transitions, Hi Henry cofounder Vedran Ismaili noticed how few companies had the right tools to support and understand their employees' wants and needs. Ismaili started talking about it with developers Fred Abrahamson and Tommy Engström, and the trio decided to create a new business tool. "The idea started with simply knowing how people are doing," Vedran said. "Looking at the market, we saw a clear need for software that was less complex and more human, so we decided to build Hi Henry to enable companies to truly be people-first."

At its core, Hi Henry is an employee-experience platform whose interface is fashioned as a friendly chatbot. From streamlined onboarding to AI-powered "smart surveys" and built-in data analysis, Hi Henry is designed to help companies build stronger relationships with their employees from day one, ultimately improving engagement, productivity and retention. Unlike the broad scope of popular virtual assistants like Apple's Siri and Amazon's Alexa, Hi Henry aims to be a role model for the niche market of employee experience. Vedran hopes Hi Henry will eventually be the perfect AI office assistant, helping new employees settle in, measuring well-being during their time at the company and giving them a proper send-off when the time comes.

[Funding History]

Bootstrap

Seed

Angel

Hi Henry bootstrapped for about six months to secure their first customers. After piquing the interest of a few early investors, the company raised €400,000 in seed funding and now has the backing of several prominent Swedish angel investors.

[Milestones]
- Incorporating the company in 2016
- Getting accepted into Stockholm's renowned Sting accelerator
- Signing our first international customer – a huge multinational corporation
- Being named one of Stockholm's hottest AI startups by angel investor Joseph Michael
- Releasing our onboarding product

[Links]
Web: **hihenry.com** Facebook: **hihenryhq** Twitter: **@HiHenryHQ** Linkedin: **company/hihenry**

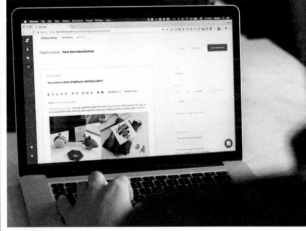

[Name]
Mentimeter

[Elevator Pitch]
"Our dream is to give every audience a voice and turn all presenters into superstars. We've created an easy-to-use software that enables interactive presentations and increased audience engagement during presentations."

[The Story]
In 2012, Johnny Warstrom and three friends from Stockholm's KTH (the Royal Institute of Technology in Stockholm) were working as consultants, educating business leaders. However, they were frustrated with the lack of tools available for creating interactive workshops and meetings, so they started to design a solution: easy-to-use software for interactive workshops and presentations that would be accessible for anyone, anywhere in the world. Focusing heavily on the product, they began building an alpha version. The positive response from friends and colleagues validated their thinking, and this was followed by securing angel investment, giving them the resources to start working full time as a team of seven in summer 2014.

Reflecting the team's commitment to being global, the whole Mentimeter team relocated to San Francisco for four months in 2016 (as part of the prestigious 500 Startups incubator, where they gained valuable insights), then, continuing to explore and embrace new cultures while escaping the Nordic darkness, they relocated to Barcelona for one month in 2017 and to Lisbon for February in 2018. International growth has been fast, and the company is currently tripling its revenue every year. Mentimeter now have customers in over one hundred countries, including many blue-chip global companies. The culturally diverse mix of twenty-one employees now incorporates sales and account-management roles, with their current challenge to manage their fast growth while remaining very product-focused.

[Funding History]

Bootstrap

Seed

Angel

Mentimeter's beta product was bootstrapped by the initial team of four, with the first outside investment coming in 2014 from four angels. During 2016, the company received further investment from 500 Startups, bringing total investment to US$500,000. By 2017, Mentimeter were already turning a profit.

[Milestones]
- Deciding to take in angel investments and taking the leap of faith to go full time
- Moving the entire team to San Francisco for the four-month 500 Startups program
- Deciding early on to have diversity as core value for the company
- Keeping the focus on product while incorporating regular customer feedback

[Links]
Web: mentimeter.com Facebook: Mentimeter Twitter: @Mentimeter Instagram: mentimeter

[Name]

NuvoAir

[Elevator Pitch]

"We combine beautiful hardware and data-collection software to improve the lives of people suffering from respiratory conditions and to streamline clinical decision making."

[The Story]

NuvoAir is an R&D innovator in respiratory healthcare technology. The startup has created two user-friendly, pocket-sized spirometers and software that links to caregivers and gives patients the ability to monitor their health from home. NuvoAir was born out of a partnership between CEO and founder Lorenzo Consoli (hailing from Novartis and Pond Innovation) and a design firm who conceptualized the first version of the spirometer (called Air Smart). Since launching their first spirometer in 2016, NuvoAir has introduced a professional app, a dashboard interface and a brand new spirometer with Bluetooth capabilities called Air Next. "We wanted to bring to market a product that was affordable, easy to use and beautifully designed, and that even patients at home could use," says Lorenzo. NuvoAir distinguishes itself in the field with their visual elements. "You finally have patients using a device that doesn't stigmatize their disease, because it looks like an object of design."

Patients using the product can seamlessly and immediately share collected data with caregivers. "More importantly," says Lorenzo, "caregivers can follow their patients' lung health anytime and have immediate access to their patients' personal data so they can focus on the most critical patients, reducing costs and improving outcomes." A mobile app that allows patients to autonomously receive insights into their lung health is also in development. According to Lorenzo, it's "a digital lung-health assistant powered by smart algorithms."

[Funding History]

Seed

In 2016, Lorenzo Consoli and a design company joined together to found NuvoAir around his vision for the innovative spirometer, with all parties becoming shareholders. In 2017, Stockholm-based VC Spiltan invested €2 million as a seed round to push both development of the product and its commercial exposure.

[Milestones]

- Receiving our seed round of €2 million from Swedish investment company Spiltan
- Signing a contract with Novartis as a distributor
- Signing a partnership with Royal Brompton Hospital to monitor cystic fibrosis patients remotely
- Launching the Bluetooth-ready Air Next spirometer

[Links]

Web: **nuvoair.com** Facebook: **NuvoAir** Twitter: **@NuvoAir** Instagram: **nuvoair**

[Name]   # Stilla

[Elevator Pitch]   *"We give you peace of mind for your belongings. The Stilla Motion unit gives you an instant notification via your phone if something moves when it shouldn't. Drop it inside your backpack or place it on top of a purse or anything else you want to protect. It keeps your valuables and loved ones secure."*

[The Story]   In 2015, while learning how to code hardware, Elin Elkehag discovered a solution to her problem of worrying about belongings when her attention was elsewhere: she accidentally dropped a test hardware board with an activated motion sensor on it. This gave her the idea of attaching a small motion-sensor unit to precious items so that if the item is moved, it sends an alarm to your phone. Failing to find such a product on the market, she decided to make it herself. She took the idea from a dream to a patent-pending hardware product in one hundred days, and Stilla Motion was born.

When the Stilla Motion unit, which can be placed inside a bag or attached to an item, is moved, it sends an instant notification to a Bluetooth-paired phone, protecting your items from loss or theft. Stilla Motion launched a crowdfunding campaign in 2016 and reached their funding goal in less than ten hours. The following summer, they shipped the first devices to paying customers in fifty-three countries. Since then, Stilla Motion has gathered a team of five passionate employees, all focused on growing the company. In 2017, they launched product sales across a major Swedish design-store chain and then across the US retail stores of telecom giant AT&T.

[Funding History]

Bootstrap   Seed   Angel

Stilla has seen investment come from seed and angel rounds, from both Swedish and US-based entrepreneurs, senior business leaders and three former NHL professionals. To date, Stilla have raised US$1.2 million, including a successful 2016 Indiegogo crowdfunding campaign.

[Milestones]
- Taking a hardware product from dream to patent pending in one hundred days
- Launching on Indiegogo crowdfunding platform in 2016 and reaching our goal in ten hours
- Growing to have paying customers in more than fifty-three countries, from Burma to Brussels
- Launching Stilla Motion in the largest telecom-operator retail store chain in the US

[Links]   Web: **wearestilla.com** Facebook: **wearestilla** Twitter: **@wearestilla** Instagram: **wearestilla**

[Name]
United Invitations

[Elevator Pitch] *"We connect natives and newcomers over home-cooked dinners in countries all over Europe in an effort to foster community and create a more open and empathic society."*

[The Story] United Invitations' founder Ebba Akerman never realized how segregated her home country of Sweden was until she started teaching the Swedish language to immigrants in Stockholm. After class, her students would often invite her over for dinner, and as they ate they'd explain to her how hard it is to learn the language when you have nobody to speak it with. Ebba decided she'd welcome her students into the Swedish community in the same way they had welcomed her into theirs: over a home-cooked meal. In 2014, she began inviting her students to have meals at her friends' homes, and these meals proved to be a success. The students said they felt more welcome in Sweden, while natives learned about a different side of their country.

Ebba built out a people-matching and booking platform to grow her idea. With the help of some positive media coverage, United Invitations began to flourish. To date, it has brought together fifteen thousand people across dinner tables in eight different European countries. Roughly fifty dinners are arranged each month on the United Invitations platform, with the goal of fostering a community that transcends borders. "We're here to fight segregation and make sure a city is a home for everyone who lives there," says Ebba.

[Funding History]

Bootstrap

External

United Invitations was bootstrapped until early 2015 when it received funding from the nonprofit Ax Foundation. United Invitations now operates as a nonprofit organization with an annual revenue of 2 million SEK. Ax Foundation continues to be United Invitations' sole financier.

[Milestones]
- Launching our business in spring of 2014
- *The New York Times* profiling us in our first year
- Receiving funding from the Ax Foundation in 2015
- Founder Ebba Akerman being invited to speak to the United Nations in Geneva in 2016

[Links] Web: **unitedinvitations.org** Facebook: **invitationsdepartementet** Twitter: **@invitationsdept**

[Name]
Watty

[Elevator Pitch]

"Our mission is about getting household energy data online and building really cool software and tools to help people make smarter energy choices and live their life in a better way."

[The Story]

When you think of global carbon emissions, you might picture smoke billowing out of factories in China or air pollution rising from a bottlenecked highway in Los Angeles, but not the emissions from your washing machine, refrigerator or other household appliances. That's what Hjalmar Nilsonne, an energy systems engineer and CEO of Watty, wants to change. His innovative product helps consumers monitor their daily household energy use and advises on how to better conserve it. Through Watty, "every home in the world can have its own energy engineer," Hjalmar says.

Watty is a small box about the size of a video-game console with clamps that attach to electrical wires to measure energy use. After installing the box, consumers receive up-to-the-minute data through the Watty app about their energy use, broken down by appliance. Users also receive tips for improving their energy use and notifications about potentially dangerous uses of energy while the house is empty; for example, a stove or appliance that's been left on. While the product launched only last summer, it has already caught the eye of major energy companies in Sweden and is being tested in the UK and Germany. "We think that every home in the world needs to be connected this way," Hjalmar says. "That would make the world a vastly better place, so that's what we're going to try to do."

[Funding History]

Bootstrap   Angel   External

A bit unconventionally, Watty hired a team of five people before raising any funding. After working on the product for a couple of months without pay, the team began raising money through sales and then received external funding from the Swedish Energy Agency and other private companies. Watty raised its first seed round of US$3.3 million from Cleantech Invest and EQT Ventures.

[Milestones]

- Launching in summer of 2017
- Being named most-efficient product out of more than forty companies in household energy space by external benchmark company
- Raising a €3 million seed round
- Making revenue that was five times higher in the first twelve weeks of 2018 than in all of 2017

[Links]

Web: **watty.io** Facebook: **wattyio** Twitter: **@Watty_io** Instagram: **watty.io**

[Name]
Worldfavor

[Elevator Pitch]
"We're a global digital platform with the mission to enable every company in the world to be sustainable and transparent. By digitalizing sustainability information, companies can track and improve their performance, share their data and analyze other companies' performance."

[The Story]
As early as 2012, Frida Emilsson and three other cofounders had seen the growing demand for transparency in how companies perform on sustainability metrics. They wanted to enable consumers to compare companies' sustainability performance in order to make more informed decisions, but sustainability reporting was often paper-based or hard to access, and because sustainability reporting was not standardized, it was hard to gather comparable data from companies. Businesses were also in need of simple tools to better manage sustainability information themselves. By 2014, Worldfavor had decided to build a platform to digitalize the world's corporate sustainability information.

Worldfavor launched its new global sustainability platform, which was based on the insights and needs of early pilot customers, in 2016. The platform makes it easier for companies to manage, visualize and share their sustainability information as well as access and evaluate other companies' information, such as suppliers or portfolio companies. With the lofty goal of having "all the world's sustainability information in one place," Worldfavor has become a leading platform and a powerful tool towards standardization of sustainability information. It now has more than thirty large enterprise customers (including well-known brands) and close to six thousand other companies from more than thirty-four countries reporting their sustainability information. Their service has created a natural network effect where customers now invite their own suppliers.

[Funding History]

Bootstrap   Seed   Angel   External

Worldfavor started out bootstrapped as the four cofounders joined resources to live and work together in a small Stockholm apartment. When Worldfavor was ready to launch their new product in 2016 and start commercializing it, it took in angel funding of €400,000 followed by €650,000 in 2017 for funding further growth.

[Milestones]
- Launching the current version of the sustainability product
- Financing rounds growing towards the first VC round backing new growth
- Relocating to its own office and expanding the team to twelve employees
- Gaining market recognition during 2017 and getting major brands as customers

[Links] Web: **worldfavor.com** Facebook: **Worldfavor** Twitter: **@worldfavor**

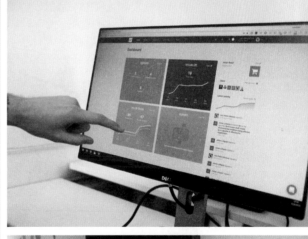

rams

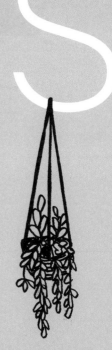

- **Create a strong team.**
  A successful startup should be comprised of a
  team with complementary skills and personalities.

- **Don't be afraid to be courageous.**
  Entrepreneurs should be stubborn and brave
  enough to stick to an initial vision, so go for it,
  even though success may not happen right away.

- **Have flexibility and patience.**
  Besides being brave, entrepreneurs need to have
  the patience and flexibility to adapt to changing
  circumstances, such as longer timeframes and
  unanticipated difficulties.

- **Attract interest from the market.**
  Create a concept that will attract interest from
  investors, users and competitors. Not only that,
  learn from the market. For instance, if you're building
  a musical instrument, work at a music store to get
  insight into how customers think.

[Name]
Amplify Sweden

[Elevator Pitch]
"We're Sweden's first MusicTech oriented startup incubator. We're taking musical creativity and technology, and remixing it with entrepreneurial excellence."

[Sector]
Music tech, tech

[Description]
Housed in the new Royal College of Music Stockholm (KMH) campus, Amplify Sweden is the first Swedish incubator to support music business and tech startups. Amplify was founded in 2017 to give these companies the opportunity to accelerate their business and be a part of Sweden's vibrant music culture. Cofounder Martin Gemvik, who has worked in VC for twenty-six years (including ten years at the renowned Sting Incubator, now one of Amplify's partners), created Amplify in conjunction with KMH, who wished to start a similar program. After only a year, Amplify has created a deal flow with KMH, partnered with Sony Music Sweden, and launched three companies.

Amplify's incubator program to support music tech growth can last six, twelve, or eighteen months, depending on the startup's maturity. "Within the frame of the program," says Martin, "members are offered various modules ranging from the basic principles of how to run a company to the universe of venture capital." Other modules include sales and pitch training, IP strategies, music industry basics and business canvas modeling. Amplify also offers high-level coaching and strategy advice. "A very important part of the incubator process is to introduce startups to the music industry, and to the logic of the music industry," says Martin.

Martin says Amplify is looking for "coachable, glowing entrepreneurs with flexible mindsets and a strong drive to be successful and fulfill their vision." Applicants should be able to present a minimum viable product, and look to be VC fundable. "The important thing here is that companies can at least sense an opportunity for a fast growing and long term profitable business," he says. Amplify encourages teams and companies to apply with an elevator pitch, and descriptions of the team, product, and market. Accepted companies don't pay the incubator upfront but instead give 4–8 percent stock warrants to Amplify. One piece of advice Martin offers prior to applying is to "try to learn from the market you're targeting, before you start spending your own money. How you do it is up to you."

[Apply to]
amplifysweden.com/contact--apply1

[Links]
Web: amplifysweden.com Facebook: amplifysweden Twitter: @AmplifySweden

 - **Have a clearly articulated problem – and a solution.**
Your product or service should address a verified
pain point within your industry.

- **Be ready to launch soon.**
Your idea should be mature, and ideally you have
a well-thought-out business plan. If not, we'll help
you get there.

- **Have a clear value proposition.**
We have a large network of investors. Your business
model should set you apart in their eyes.

- **Think big.**
Your startup should have global market potential,
and you should be thinking about international
applications for your technology.

- **Be able to think fast.**
During the program, you'll have to build fast
and pivot even faster.

- **Be unique.**
We're looking for startups with one-of-a-kind tech
solutions, especially with IoT applications or a focus
on 5G applications.

[Name]
Ericsson ONE

[Elevator Pitch]
"We're a global community of thinkers and doers – designers, developers and entrepreneurs – connected by a shared mission to create easy innovations that scale, last and solve real problems. We believe in experimentation and hands-on learning by doing."

[Sector]
Innovation, tech, network, communication

[Description]
Ericsson ONE is the open innovation platform and incubator within the Swedish multinational telecom giant Ericsson. With nearly 40 percent market share in the telecom industry and a track record stretching back to 1876, Ericsson wields a time-tested network of investors, academics and industry experts, all of whom can help new companies find the market fit that allows them to scale internationally. The incubator program offers startups the opportunity for global testing and experimentation with their products, services and ideas, and also provides access to deep insights in Ericsson's technological areas of expertise such as 5G and the rapidly growing realm of the Internet of Things (IoT).

The incubator works with two groups of startup companies per year, with each cohort receiving six months of tailored coaching and action-oriented mentoring. Startups are connected to real customer cases and, through joint seminars and workshops, are able to expand their teams' skill sets and grow their networks. The incubator program works with participating startups to create clear goals and milestones and to provide them with the opportunity to work with Ericsson itself as their first customer. For new companies without previous clients, this can be an important step in securing real customer case studies for future use. The program also provides additional business-development support to its selected startups and facilitates access to a range of industry-leading corporations and potential investors. Ericsson ONE is particularly well positioned to facilitate market exposure for new companies, regardless of size.

The program accepts startups in all stages of development. Whether searching for an initial customer, building and fine-tuning a new technology, or scaling a potentially world-changing idea, Ericsson ONE is ready to offer support. The program's ethos is all about cocreation and finding synergies where startups and Ericsson can benefit from each other, so startups with applications in 5G and IoT are especially encouraged to apply.

[Apply to]
Matilda George / matilda.george@ericsson.com

Online / ericsson.com/en/ericsson-one/for-start-ups

[Links]
Web: ericsson.com/en/ericsson-one Facebook: ericsson Twitter: @ericsson

- **Share the Foodtech Village mission.**
  Your startup should align with our three central themes: good for you, good for the planet, and good for your taste buds.

- **Be ready to showcase your work.**
  Foodtech Village members get priority access to highly-coveted spots at some of Sweden's biggest food and tech events such as Smaka på Stockholm, Gastronord and Sweden Demo Day.

- **Be prepared to scale up.**
  We have a long list of corporate and VC partners ready to work with up-and-coming foodtech companies.

- **Fix something.**
  We believe the current food system is broken, and we're looking for innovators who address shortcomings within the industry, no matter how small.

- **Collaborate.**
  Improving the food system is all about working together. Wherever you fit into the picture, be open to unexpected partnerships with researchers, investors and other startups.

[Name] Foodtech Village

[Elevator Pitch] *"We help foodtech and agtech startups reach their full potential by providing access to our corporate and VC partners and by sharing our expertise in emerging technologies. We also promote the Swedish foodtech scene through events and conferences."*

[Sector] **Foodtech, sustainability, innovative agriculture, supply chain, gastronomy, waste management, personal health**

[Description] Foodtech Village is a community of people who are passionate about working towards better food, a better food industry, and ultimately a better world. Following the adage "It takes a village to raise a child," Foodtech Village supports entrepreneurs at the intersection of food and technology by connecting them with corporations, researchers, governments and investors interested in the same issues. As part of the Sweden Foodtech umbrella organization, Foodtech Village aims to make Stockholm a global hub for foodtech and to transform the food sector more broadly through digital innovation and entrepreneurship.

A key aspect of Foodtech Village is its CrowdFood Accelerator, designed to help promising foodtech startups develop their value proposition, fine-tune their products and launch large-scale crowdfunding campaigns. The accelerator is a six-month, bootcamp-style program covering vision and product development, marketing, pitching and negotiating, team leadership, legal assistance and financial planning. Foodtech Village also offers a range of networking events, including monthly meetups and biannual Big Meets, and it organizes a showcase of foodtech companies during Stockholm's annual food festival Smaka på (Taste of Stockholm). They also participate in the Gastronord food industry trade show, the Swedish political forum Almedalen Week and the Sweden Demo Day "un-conference" for tech entrepreneurs.

Foodtech Village is always on the lookout for innovators who use technology to improve the food system. Any startups addressing issues in the food industry – from using science to improve produce yields or to reduce fossil fuel use during distribution, to bringing cutting-edge gadgets to consumers and chefs – are welcome to apply. This includes companies that design and develop new food products, improve existing products, or research industry trends. Foodtech Village members also benefit from the Sweden Foodtech Center, the program's sister space in central Stockholm. Acting as a test-bed for new food-related innovations, the center showcases cooking labs, urban farms and zero-waste structures, among other sustainability initiatives.

[Apply to] team@swedenfoodtech.com

- **Understand the customer's needs and validate the problem that needs to be solved.**
  Great startups get out of the basement
  to understand and assess existing problems
  and existing solutions.

- **Show an understanding of yourself.**
  Investors will ask why you're suited for your startup,
  so make sure you can call upon your own experience
  to answer. Even better, find a cofounder with
  complementary strengths to support your personal
  and company identity.

- **Have passion for the problem.**
  Love your area of work and the problem faced rather
  than a specific technology or solution, which will
  likely change over the lifespan of a company
  (while the focus on a problem will not).

- **Prepare to be persistent.**
  Have endurance and a lasting passion in the field
  instead of wanting to make a quick buck. Be prepared
  to live a year without funding or a salary. Patience will
  make you a better founder.

[Name]
Founder Institute

[Elevator Pitch] *"In just fourteen weeks, our Founder Institute program accelerates the development of your company with mentoring by serial entrepreneurs, a structured development agenda, and connections to the right network, equaling a year's worth of progress."*

[Sector] **Web technology, digital**

[Description] Created for passionate entrepreneurs, the Founder Institute is an intensive accelerator program that provides practical training and mentoring. Participants undergo fourteen weeks of rigorous work with the goal of graduating as founders well on their way to success. "We support founders with structured company-building work," said Joel Sunnehall, the director of Founder Institute and founder of Desifer, the company that runs the Founder Institute. "We connect them with really highly specialized mentors who are serial entrepreneurs themselves." Special care is also taken to foster corporate connections.

Founders enrolled in the program dig into important topics, such as getting funding, developing and launching a product, and validating the needs of the customer. In only three and a half months, founders go from idea phase to pitching to mentors, building the team, developing a major pitch, raising funds and launching to the market. Part of the program includes committing to creating a company, if the founders haven't already. In addition, founders commit to a fifteen-year warrant, giving the cohort 4 percent of the founders' companies. This is divided so that mentors share 1 percent, Desifer receives 1 percent, the Institute HQ receives 1 percent, and the graduates share the remaining 1 percent. "Everyone in the local ecosystem is incentivized to help build successful companies," says Joel.

"The Founder Institute is looking for founders who are passionate about solving a certain problem," he says. This passion should ideally be in solving a problem rather than focusing on a technology-specific solution, such as blockchain. "You can be almost certain that a solution will change throughout the lifetime of a startup." To apply for the Institute, individual candidates and teams must pass an online evaluation and in-person interview. Future founders should focus especially on an unresolved customer need and demonstrate a minimum of eight years of work experience, preferably in a field corresponding to solving that problem or need.

[Apply to] fi.co/join

[Links] Web: **fi.co/home** Facebook: **FounderInstitute** Twitter: **@founding** Instagram: **founding**

- **Be open to new challenges.**
  This is the most important for success!
  We only accept people who are open to learning
  new things and ideas.

- **Enjoy learning in new environments.**
  Our students embrace learning by doing. You'll work
  on real-world cases and spend time outside of the
  classroom; it's part of our lifelong learning philosophy.

- **Thrive in a collaborative environment.**
  We encourage knowledge-sharing within schools so
  that students can learn together and from each other.

- **Be excited about leading by example.**
  We develop leadership and self-confidence in our
  students so you can challenge the status quo when
  you go into the professional world.

- **Be willing to move to Stockholm.**
  Our programs are in Stockholm but are taught
  in English, and students come from different
  nationalities and experiences.

[Name]
Hyper Island

[Elevator Pitch]
"We design learning experiences that challenge companies and individuals to grow and stay competitive in an increasingly digitized world. Our programs and courses seek to provide the knowledge and skills to lead change and begin a journey of lifelong learning."

[Sector]
Creative

[Description]
"A school for entrepreneurs is a byproduct of what we do, but not the only focus," says Karin Engman Carlsson, director of Hyper Island School, Sweden. Their main goal is to build strong individuals who can challenge the status quo through experience-based learning and then go into the business world and create positive change. Hyper Island's 4,500 alumni can speak to this. In 1996, the three founders realized that technology was having a huge impact both on people and on how they learn. The traditional classroom environment meant people couldn't learn and unlearn fast enough. Hyper Island was founded to provide the tools needed for lifelong learning and for keeping up with the rapidly changing digital landscapes of technology and leadership.

There are two main tracks available at Hyper Island in Stockholm: vocational training, where entrance is based on a person's potential rather than grades; and master's programs, where a bachelor's degree and work experience is required. Programs help students develop a range of in-demand workplace skills including digital acceleration, social media and data. The business developer programs focus on the skills needed for both intrapreneurship and entrepreneurship. "You don't have to be incredible," says Samuel Hedberg, program manager of the Digital Media Creative Program, "you just have to be open. Everybody chooses their own specialization and career path. We let people focus on their own topics." There are also shorter programs offered throughout the year, including the Hyper Island Way Course, where individuals learn about the Hyper Island toolbox in a three-day crash course.

These days, Hyper Island's Swedish business partners know they need a corporate mindset change to survive in an increasingly competitive world, and they come to Hyper Island for it. Some businesses, amazed by the Hyper Island alumni who work for their organizations, ask for custom programs designed to tackle their business challenges and needs. It's all about embracing change.

[Apply to]
hyperisland.com

[Links]
Web: **hyperisland.com** Facebook: **hyperisland** Twitter: **@hyperisland** Instagram: **hyperisland**

- Be looking for your first large customer.
  We can help if you're looking for a strategic partner,
  not a sponsor. Startups looking to validate their
  business model or product are perfect.

- Know the value you bring to the table.
  We help set up the meetings with corporates
  in the program, but you should know the value
  you can bring to the table.

- Have a scalable business model.
  We welcome mostly B2B startups, based on our
  partners' interests, with a scalable business model
  and developed product.

- Intend to be based in Sweden and do business here.
  We're here to help Swedish-based early-stage
  startups succeed in the short and long term.

- Be an unlisted startup.
  We can only work with private startups, preferably
  younger than five years. Most companies usually
  have around four employees including the founders.

[Name]	# Ignite Sweden

[Elevator Pitch]

"We're the home of startup-corporate collaboration in Sweden. We help startups find their first large customers by connecting them to the right stakeholders at the right corporate. We also help corporates become more startup friendly."

[Sector]

Corporate matchmaking

[Description]

Ignite Sweden is a collaborative program part-owned by some of Sweden's leading early-stage startup supporters, THINGS, STING, LEAD, MINC and Uminova Innovation in collaboration with SISP. The program is funded in part by Vinnova, the Swedish government's innovation arm. Since launching in February 2017, they have facilitated 1,065 meetings between startups and corporates and worked with around 230 startups and 55 corporate partners.

The aim of the Ignite Sweden program is to validate the business model and technology of B2B startups and quickly prove their scalability by taking care of corporate introductions and organizational navigation. A successful outcome of the program is a commercial trial or signed contract between the startup and corporate. There's no cost for startups to participate and no investment provided. Before the corporate meetings, startups are provided with a sales toolset and are offered a thirty-minute coaching session by some of Sweden's best startup sales coaches. The Ignite Sweden team follows the ongoing relationship closely to make sure discussions lead to paid collaborations, and they also have a team ready to help startups get through corporate legal and procurement processes. As Stina Lantz, project manager of Ignite Sweden at THINGS said, "You can't truly know if the business is scalable until your first client."

All startup applications are screened when new corporate partnerships are established, so everyone has an equal chance of being selected. The online application takes about ten minutes to complete. As an entrepreneur herself, Stina knows how valuable a first paid client can be. She believes startups will never be sure whether the problem they're solving is big enough if they provide things for free. Plus, a paid partnership can do wonders when going to raise money. "It's a great thing to get your first customer before your first funding," Stina says. "If you can prove customer traction, your funding pitch is stronger."

[Apply to]

ignitesweden.org/startups

[Links]

Web: **ignitesweden.org** Twitter: **@IgniteSweden**

- **Be early stage.**
  We provide the resources that KTH students
  and researchers need in order to make new
  discoveries and develop new technologies before
  building them up to enter the world of business.

- **Be focused on science and technology.**
  It's important that you're making use of our
  resources to make new breakthroughs and
  prepare them for the market.

- **Have a desire to make an impact**
  Your new technology or scientific research
  should have the goal of making a meaningful,
  lasting positive impact on society at large.

- **You or your team members are studying
  or researching at KTH.**
  We're a resource for KTH students and
  researchers. For that reason, at least half of your
  founding team must be enrolled as students
  or researchers at KTH in order to qualify.

[Name] # KTH Innovation

[Elevator Pitch] *"We're the Innovation unit and pre-incubator at the KTH Royal Institute of Technology, Sweden's largest technical and engineering university. Our mission is to develop groundbreaking technologies and bring them to market where they can make a meaningful impact on society."*

[Sector] **Research and development**

[Description] As a part of KTH Royal Institute of Technology, also known as the "MIT of Stockholm," KTH Innovation is an impactful pre-incubator where professors, researchers and students collaborate to make new scientific and technological breakthroughs in the fields of renewable energy, biotech, medtech, ICT hardware and software, cleantech, and material science, among others. KTH's Swedish university roots make it a standout among both incubators and academic institutions alike. Although typically intellectual property from discoveries made in university labs belong to that university, individual professors in Sweden own the IP rights to their discoveries. KTH Innovation also offers unique opportunities for students who want to get their tech out into the world as quickly and capably as possible. Inspired by the Third Mission, a European movement to add positive societal engagement to universities' two traditional missions (teaching and research), KTH Innovation takes no equity in the projects it jumpstarts, and it provides an array of resources, from legal counsel and funding to labs and office space. As a result, much of the tech developed at KTH Innovation may not have emerged were it not for this unique incentive structure.

KTH Innovation projects are as diverse as they are numerous, thanks to the university's five different technical schools. "Some of our most innovative research comes out of very niche disciplines, such as wood science," says Program and Community Manager Nicole Forsberg. Every year, KTH Innovation supports approximately three hundred new ideas from researchers and students by offering resources such as patent support, specialized business coaching in various fields of technology, soft funding, investor matchmaking, and pre-incubation. When it comes to setting important benchmarks, the pre-incubator's acceleration process for startups aims to fast-track their time to market. KTH Innovation support is available for active KTH researchers and students, and is completely confidential and free of charge. To be eligible, at least 50 percent of your founding team must be active researchers or KTH students.

[Apply to] **innovation@kth.se**

[Links] Web: kth.se/en/innovation Facebook: kthinnovation Twitter: @kthinnovation

- **Have at least one SSES student or alumni on your team.**
  You must have a minimum of two persons on the team, of which at least one must be a student or alumni at one of the five SSES member universities or be involved in SSES activities in other related ways.

- **Have vision.**
  You must address a challenge that has a high level of complexity and involves multiple disciplines. Be prepared to focus exclusively.

- **You must not be enrolled in any another acceleration programs or plan to enroll in any others.**
  You may reside off-site and continue to do so throughout your Affinity acceleration.

- **Have an idea with great potential and/or social value.**
  The service or product must have solid business potential and/or a clear and positive social impact.

[Name]

SSES Ventures: Affinity

[Elevator Pitch]

"Our goal is to empower high-performing individuals during their entrepreneurial journey. Affinity is designed to complete the conventional acceleration process by providing tailor-made resources, connecting interdisciplinary minds, and otherwise directly supporting companies in their growth."

[Sector] **Industry-agnostic**

[Description]

Affinity exists at the peak of the acceleration process for high-potential seed-stage startups in Stockholm. It has is origins in the alumni community of the Stockholm School of Entrepreneurship (SSES), where bold ideas conceived during courses quickly gathered steam to become real, thriving enterprises. As time passed, the SSES Launchpad for effective startups became more and more fine-tuned, until it took the form of the Affinity Accelerator. Affinity is supported by an enthusiastic, enlightened and well-connected community of experts who provide teams with the tools they need to take their ideas to the next level – with no strings attached. Affinity does not take equity from the companies it incubates, and it exists primarily as a support network where people can quickly iterate, collaborate and grow. This is achieved through a very careful selection process. Each year, only ten startups are selected to join the program.

At Affinity, entrepreneurs codesign their dream acceleration path and are granted an array of resources as well as high-profile advisors to help execute their vision. The advanced interdisciplinary environment is ideal for motivated individuals who already have some traction with their startups and who are seeking successful ways to achieve their larger strategic vision, and to do so in an advanced interdisciplinary environment. Though Affinity does not follow a traditionally structured program, they do believe strongly in generous, personalized support. Entrepreneurs are asked what they want to achieve, and are then offered assistance with everything from intellectual property rights and legal service to digitization, leadership and internationalization.

Affinity also has office space as well as a robust network of affiliates that offer the entrepreneurs whatever support they need for up to one and a half years. This is of huge importance to the startups, which typically have some form of investment already but no finalized product. That, however, changes fast, thanks to a diverse network of leaders in business, engineering, design and academia.

[Apply to] sses.se/ventures/accelerator

[Links] Web: **sses.se/ventures** Facebook: **ssesupdates** Twitter: **@SSESupdates** Instagram: **lifeatsses**

- **Have a strong team.**
  We look very closely at the team, and though we'll help you find the right candidates as you grow, you need a team of at least two founders with a strong tech and business development skills, and at least one of them must be working full time with the startup.

- **Have a strong idea that solves a clear problem.**
  We need to see some kind of proof that there's a need for the product you're working on and that it solves a specific problem.

- **Have a strong digital approach.**
  Your idea needs to be based on innovative technology.

- **Have a strong prototype.**
  You need to have launched a prototype to apply for our programs.

[Name]	# Sting

[Elevator Pitch]
"We're the leading accelerator and incubator in the Nordic countries. We've been running our programs since 2002, and during the past fifteen years we've worked with more than 240 companies, of which 70 percent are still active."

[Sector]
Digital startups

[Description]
Sting calls itself the leading accelerator and incubator in Scandinavia, but some would argue that it's much more than that: Sting provides a whole ecosystem for the startup scene in Stockholm and beyond. It currently offers four main programs for startups called Incubate, Accelerate, Open Coaching and Test Drive, thus offering services to young startups as well as to more experienced ones. The selected startups are provided with many services, ranging from coaching to help with PR, hiring candidates and finding investors.

The most popular feature is the individual coaching, which puts the startup in the driver's seat by being based on the pull rather than push method: no answers are given, but all the necessary questions are asked. All coaches are former entrepreneurs or venture capitalists. Another popular aspect of the programs is the networking opportunity. More than 240 startups have gone through Sting's programs, and as 70 percent of them are still active there's a large community of more experienced entrepreneurs at hand for the new participants. On top of the individual coaching and networking opportunities, Sting offers relevant courses, workshops and breakfast seminars to help the startups find their place and people in the ecosystem.

Sting focuses on digital startups, especially those in ICT, games, medtech/health, cleantech and sustainability. The Incubate program provides startups with the chance of an investment of just under €30,000, while those selected for the Accelerator program automatically receive that investment. Sting reserves the right to sign a stock option corresponding to 2 to 6 percent of the shares in the startups (2 percent for the Accelerate program and 6 percent for the Incubate program), but the stock option will be diluted once the startup begins to raise capital on its own. Sting Incubate runs three batches per year with approximately five startups in each batch, while Sting Accelerate runs twice a year with eight startups in each batch.

[Apply to]
sting.co/en/apply

[Links]
Web: **sting.co/en** Facebook: **stingsthlm** Twitter: **@stingsthlm** Instagram: **stingsthlm**

ces

A house

[Name]

[Address] Östermalmsgatan 26A, 114 26 Stockholm

[Total Area]

12,000м²

[Workspaces]

400

[The Story] A house was founded in 2015 by a group of creative entrepreneurs who believed that innovation, at its core, is about networking and dialogue. The building itself is the former home of a well-known architecture school and is still owned by Akademiska Hus, Sweden's state-owned real estate company tasked with developing academic properties. The five-story brutalist structure has always been provocative – it was even dubbed the "ugliest building in Stockholm" – and A house wants to "recycle and reinvent" the radical history of the building. The space caters to startups and individuals within the food, fashion and media industries, and members are often connected by common themes of environmental sustainability, circular economies and trade.

As a "members' house" (not just a coworking space), A house offers an energetic lobby, solo workstations and studios up to 600 m², along with perks such as annual parties, weekly yoga classes and free breakfast every Thursday. Their transdisciplinary member base ranges from individual freelancers and consultants to larger companies and teams. A house also boasts a spectrum of event spaces, including a kitchen lab, an auditorium and a film studio, all available for rent by the hour, day, week or month. And they aren't stopping there: they've got a 1,000 m² stage opening soon, along with a restaurant, a brewery and professional music studios.

[Links] Web: ahousestockholm.com Facebook: ahousestockholm Instagram: ahousestockholm

Face of the Space:

Tua Asplund is CEO and partner
of A house. After working for years in
the hotel industry and getting her BA in
business administration, Tua took over her
father's printing business and consulted
for A house during the initial stages, later
joining the team on a permanent basis.
Tua's passion lies in the intersection
of business, creativity and placemaking,
so   A house was a natural fit.

[Name] # Alma

[Address] Nybrogatan 8, 114 34 Stockholm

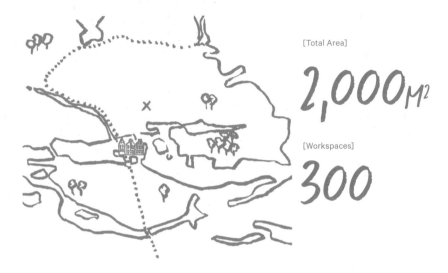

[Total Area]

2,000M²

[Workspaces]

300

[The Story] Alma was started by entrepreneurs Anna Behring Lundh and Fredrik Carlström, whose time working together in Stockholm some two decades ago inspired them to join forces later down the line. In 2016, after noticing there was a lack of work spaces for creatives to collaborate, they opened their doors to the public. But Alma is more than just a coworking space. Housed in a former design college, the members' club preserves the original five-story structure's quirks and pays tribute to both international and Scandinavian design. Its bold, dark interiors are balanced out by a glass-roofed atrium that allows natural light to flood in. The atrium is the heart of Alma; not only does it lie at the center of the structure's two buildings, it's also a restaurant and venue where Alma's exhibitions and events are held.

In addition to the communal and private work spaces available, Alma also has a music studio, an outdoor terrace and spaces specifically designed for social interactions. This means that whether members need meeting rooms, down time or opportunities to get inspired from others, it's all at their fingertips. The kinds of people at Alma work across a range of industries, such as tech, film, journalism and art, to name a few. It is truly a space "for creatives, by creatives."

[Links] Web: **thisisalma.com** Facebook: **welcometoalma** Instagram: **welcometoalma**

Face of the Space:
Alma CEO Anna Behring Lundh worked
with her now-cofounder Fredrik Carlström
at an ad agency in the late 1990s. With
many years of experience in marketing
communications under her belt, she
launched Alma in 2016. A major aspect
to her role involves connecting members
and nourishing their ideas.

[Name] # Goto 10

[Address]   Hammarby Kaj 10D, 120 07 Stockholm

[Total Area]

900M²

[Workspaces]

90

[The Story]   Goto 10 is the result of a long tradition of innovation promotion at the Internet
Foundation in Sweden (IIS), an independent organization that acts to ensure
the development of the internet and internet usage in Sweden. The Goto 10 space
opened in May 2017 in the same building as the IIS's new offices, and quickly became
a hub of knowledge exchange by hosting events ranging from talks on internet history
and culture to workshops on 3D-printing and programming.

The glass building is located on Hammarby Kaj, so those working in the lounge can
enjoy ample light and a view of the waterfront. As you enter, you're welcomed by
an imaginatively assembled robot, and inside you'll find decor that combines fractal
shapes, neon lights and technology, a variety of art pieces, a Lego wall, and even
an arcade machine. The space, characterized by a mixture of futuristic and retro
features, encourages creativity and play. There's also the SWAJ Krubb & Kafé,
a partner who offers delicious breakfast, fika, and lunch.

The Goto 10 coworking space is located on the second floor and promotes
internet-related projects at an early stage by subsidizing office space for a limited
amount of time. It's a welcoming, collaborative environment with the focus on
knowledge exchange for increased innovation. Membership is free, and members
are offered spaces to organize lectures, workshops and networking events.

[Links]   Web: goto10.se Facebook: goto10se Twitter: @goto10se Instagram: goto10se

Face of the Space:

Isadora Hellegren leads the work of Goto 10, and her interests lie in various aspects of knowledge sharing and internet-specific technologies, culture and governance. She's the author of "A History of Crypto-Discourse: Encryption as a Site of Struggles to Define Internet Freedom" (2017), and she holds a research-oriented M.A. in Communication Studies from McGill University. She's also an elected member of the Global Internet Governance Academic Network (GigaNet) Steering Committee.

[Name] # H2 Health Hub

[Address] Hälsingegatan 45, 113 31 Stockholm

[Total Area]

1,300M²

[Workspaces]

130

[The Story] Since opening in early 2016, H2 Health Hub has evolved into the preferred meeting place for the health-tech community in Stockholm. Health-tech startups often venture into uncharted territories as they try to integrate their solutions into preexisting healthcare systems, and they face a number of specific challenges such as regulatory issues, data storage concerns and the choice of business models. H2 Health Hub was established to create a coworking space where people could work, collaborate and create to not only overcome these challenges but also share experiences and build new ecosystems together, says Paul Beatus, CEO and cofounder. Perhaps the biggest benefit enjoyed by the startups are the synergies created by the close interaction between startups, partners and the network of international companies (including Samsung, Pfizer and Bonnier), all representing different business sectors that will play major roles in the future health ecosystem.

H2, which is located in an old auction house in the life-science cluster of the emerging area Hagastaden, offers both flexible and designated workstations, event space and conference rooms. Recently, it also expanded next door to provide a quiet space, library and tech lab for its members. To help build community, encourage collaboration and innovation, and stimulate the growth of the ecosystem, H2 hosts both public and private events such as community breakfasts and investor mingles, and also invites inspirational speakers.

[Links] Web: h2healthhub.com Facebook: h2HealthHub Twitter: @h2Hub Instagram: h2healthhub

Face of the Space:

Johanna Cederroth has been with H2 as the community manager since the beginning. Her previous experience from the broadcasting industry, as it was going through the throes of digitalization and implementing new technical solutions, made her leap to the health-tech scene easy. Her role at H2 is to help create the environment and network opportunities so members can continue building the value chains needed for the success of the health tech sector.

WAKE UP.
KICK ASS.
REPEAT.

Impact Hub Stockholm

[Name]

[Address]   Luntmakargatan 25, 111 37, Stockholm

[Total Area]

250M²

[Workspaces]

40

[The Story]   "Anyone can be an entrepreneur, but how do we make sure the businesses we create benefit people and planet? How can we promote collaboration to maximize our collective impact?" These are questions Jesper Kjellerås, founder and managing director of Impact Hub Stockholm, set out to answer. And in fifteen years, his vision hasn't changed. The idea was always to create a community for innovation at the intersection of meaning, disciplines and cultures, and to create positive change for our world. Thousands have called Impact Hub Stockholm home, and each one was accepted based on their individual values and knowledge. The community welcomes everyone, and celebrates the zebras of startups over the unicorns.

You won't find a receptionist at the entrance, but you'll be greeted by a community host, one of whose many jobs is to help members make meaningful connections within the community. The space offers flex desk workspaces, a terrace with three-hundred-person capacity, showers, bike lockers and two internal conference rooms. This centrally-located home-away-from-home was designed not merely with the members in mind but by the members themselves. "It goes beyond just the furniture and the walls," says Jesper. Impact Hub Stockholm also hosts many international events, including some organized by the Swedish Government, whose purpose goes beyond a positive financial return.

[Links]   Web: **impacthub.se** Facebook: **ImpactHubStockholm** Twitter: **@ImpactHubSTO**

Face of the Space:

Jesper Kjellerås cofounded one of the first coworking spaces in Stockholm in 2005 and joined the Hub Network in 2008. The Hub rebranded in 2013 to Impact Hub Stockholm, with Jesper as the founder and managing director. Jesper's experience includes corporate change-management consulting, mentoring EU startups and being a judge for social innovation and sustainability awards, including Coompanion's Cooperative of the Year award and Vinnova's Challenge Driven Innovation program.

[Name]
Norrsken House

[Address]   Birger Jarlsgatan 57 C, 113 56 Stockholm

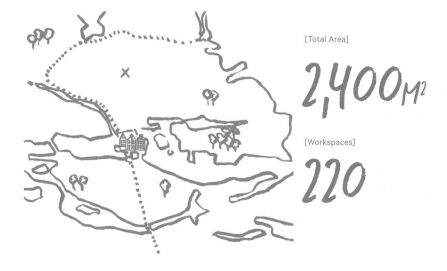

[Total Area]

2,400m²

[Workspaces]

220

[The Story]   The Norrsken Foundation was launched in 2016 when Niklas Adalberth of Klarna decided to start something that would have a positive impact on the world. While looking for a small office space for the nascent project, the founding team came across a former tram warehouse in downtown Stockholm and decided to scale up their idea to match the grandeur of the building. Accompanied by a specialized investment arm under the Norrsken Foundation umbrella, Norrsken House officially opened its doors in June 2017 with the mission of fostering socially and environmentally conscious entrepreneurship. Now the coworking space is home to over one hundred companies, from tech startups to more traditional nonprofits and NGOs.

The highly selective Norrsken House offers special subsidies to companies with a strong social mission. All members enjoy a discounted rate on event space rentals and free entry to Norrsken's in-house events, including fireside chats with prominent tech influencers. The coworking space itself comes complete with meeting rooms, Skype booths, quiet areas, a fully operational photography studio, a vegan café and even a kids' playroom. Norrsken House also coordinates weekly office hours and workshops with more than thirty partners, from law firms to investors to tech experts and corporations.

[Links]   Web: norrskenhouse.org Facebook: norrskenfoundation Twitter: @norrsken_org

Face of the Space:

Oskar Malm Wiklund is head of Member Experience and Tech at Norrsken House. While studying creative digital media at Hyper Island, he cofounded his own community-building and management company, Conneqtify. Oskar joined the Norrsken team in 2017, bringing with him his passion for socially responsible business.

> Phone [...]
> Library
> Meditation Room
> Town Hall

> Studio
> Post Office

Conference Rooms >

Skype Rooms

Openlab

[Name]

[Address] Valhallavägen 79, 114 28 Stockholm

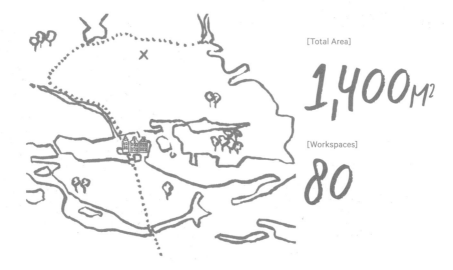

[Total Area]

1,400m²

[Workspaces]

80

[The Story] Openlab launched in 2013 as a result of seven partners in the Stockholm region coming together for one common goal: to find new and innovative approaches to solving society's challenges. Those partners – the City of Stockholm, Stockholm County Council, Stockholm County Administrative Board, KTH Royal Institute of Technology, Stockholm University, Södertörn University and the Karolinska Institute – developed the space by bringing together people from different disciplines and professions into a challenge-driven innovation community. The Openlab team are process experts in transforming the public sector through user-centered design and digital innovation, and they provide onsite courses for professionals and master's students.

Openlab is housed in the former dean's building of KTH, where three floors have been repurposed for its activities. The Open Café provides visitors with certified-organic, multicultural food, and the conference center close to the entrance includes a multi-purpose hall, several workshops and flexible spaces for smaller groups. Openlab membership is a mixture of full-time and part-time members on all floors. The decor has a light and open feel, and there are plenty of whiteboards for jotting down and sharing ideas. It's a down-to-earth and unpretentious environment with lots of prototyping and exploration going on. The Openlab team and community members all have the same working conditions and are all blended together into the creative space.

[Links] Web: openlabsthlm.se Facebook: OpenlabSthlm Instagram: openlabsthlm

Face of the Space:

Ida Niskanen, Openlab's communications manager, is a graduate from Openlabs own master's course. Formerly, she studied development and international cooperation, focusing on solving societal challenges on a global level. Her interests have always been around sustainability topics, and she has worked with several nonprofit organizations. Alongside her current communication role at Openlab, she's also coordinator of the digital ideation platform called developyourcity.com.

[Name] STHLM Music City

[Address] The Royal College of Music, Valhallavägen 105, 115 51 Stockholm

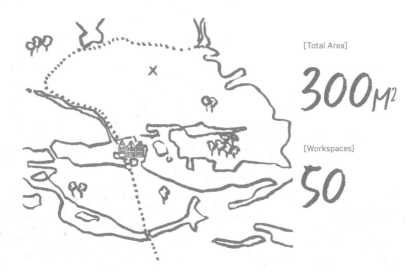

[Total Area]

300M²

[Workspaces]

50

[The Story] The founders of STHLM Music City describe their venture as a community for music creators, innovators, tech companies and more. STHLM Music City utilizes spaces in Stockholm and other startup hub cities. To facilitate and support communication and collaboration across industries, it connects "all the hubs globally where we already work," says founder and initiator Sara Herrlin. The community was created to be what the founding partners call an "all-access pass" to raise the quality of connections made between companies and individuals and to bring the music industry into the startup ecosystem.

STHLM Music City's main Stockholm space is housed in the new Royal College of Music (KMH) campus and is a member company of the incubator Amplify. The founders maintain a casual and close-knit feeling of home for their members. Both there and abroad, their community model includes subscription-based networking and events with yearly meetups, events and many other opportunities to connect creators, startups and investors. "We're more like WeWork in membership," says Sara, "working with existing tech hubs in all categories to touch music and creatives." Their content and community has seen an engagement of 350,000 people and is still growing, both in person and virtually. This makes STHLM Music City both a leading voice in music tech and an umbrella uniting important figures and their respective industries.

[Links] Web: **sthlmmusic.se** Facebook: **sthlmmusic** Twitter: **@sthlmmusic** Instagram: **sthlmmusic**

Face of the Space:

Sara Herrlin is a music industry professional, formerly of Virgin Music, who has brought her experience into the startup world. She's a founder of STHLM Music City and a principal initiator in their international community. With a background in the music industry, Sara works to inspire innovative communication between music creators, professionals in music technology, and tech startups.

[Name] # SUP46

[Address] Regeringsgatan 65, 3f, 111 56, Stockholm

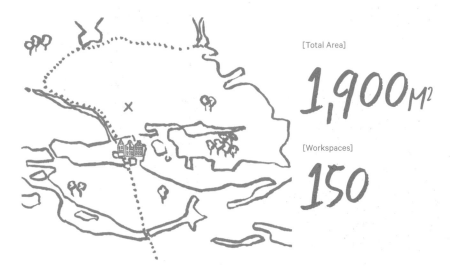

[Total Area]

1,900M²

[Workspaces]

150

[The Story] SUP46 (Startup People of Sweden), a coworking space and international hub
for early-stage tech companies, was founded in 2013 by Jessica Stark, Sebastian
Fuchs and Nathalie Nylén with the goal of fostering strong networks and community.
Accepted startups receive a broad range of support, and members both help and
invest in one another, leading to what community manager Sonia Karaugh calls a pool
of knowledge. "The ecosystem really feeds back," she says. "It's very founder-friendly.
We offer them support and mentorship in a variety of areas, such as fundraising,
international expansion, PR and communications, recruitment and much more." SUP46
is selective about applicants, and successful members are asked to make room for
newer startups once they reach ten staff members or their A funding round.

The modern facility, housed in a former Deutsche Bank building, offers amenities
such as a hangout lounge, community breakfasts, ping-pong and foosball tables,
and a cafe/workspace that's also open to non-members. Coworking options include
flex seats, flex desks, private offices, meeting rooms, and conference spaces,
and remote membership is possible too. SUP46 is inherently welcoming and helpful;
for example, it provides members with detailed maps of both the space itself and of
Sweden showing how to find all the founders, and SUP46 alumni sometimes become
angel investors in companies entering their coworking alma mater, making SUP46
more of a community than simply a physical space.

[Links] Web: sup46.com Facebook: SUP46 Twitter: @SUP_46 Instagram: sup_46

Face of the Space:
Sonia Kaurah, as SUP46's community
manager, is the first point of contact for
startups as well as alumni companies in
their international network. She also works
with corporate partners to help connect
with SUP46 startups. Originally trained in
nutrition, Sonia got her start in the startup
world in her native Australia as part of an
entrepreneurial family, before crossing
the globe to Sweden.

[Name]   # The Park

[Address]   Hälsingegatan 49, 113 31 Stockholm

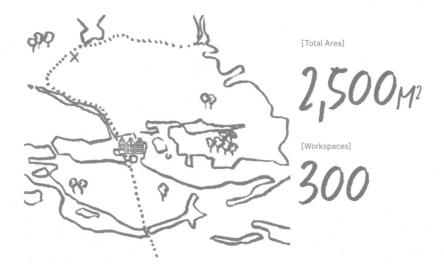

[Total Area]

2,500M²

[Workspaces]

300

[The Story]   The Park's history was forged in January 2002 when digital media entrepreneur Mikael Ahlström needed more space to grow his digital agency. This was the earliest era for coworking spaces, and he realized the benefits of a networked office space where his company could cohabitate with freelancers and other contributors. From there, The Park was created. It now consists of two locations in central Stockholm – Sveavägen 98 with its 'corporate New York' vibe, and the larger Hälsingegatan 49 venue with 'bouncing Berlin' as the theme. The Park prides itself on its soft values and on taking care of people. The welcoming and personal coworking space is all about the people, where everything has been created with heart to make people feel good and cared about while focusing on their businesses.

The Hälsingegatan space, located in an old mineral water factory from the early 1930s, retains its industrial character with high ceilings and big windows, while the expansive one-level floor space shows lots of color and is warmly decorated. The Park offers four levels of membership: Room, Fulltime, Mobile, and Lounge, with services based on the individual and company needs at the time. Members of The Park become part of a wider network with over five hundred entrepreneurs of all ages distributed among two hundred companies active in all possible industries.

[Links]   Web: thepark.se Facebook: thepark.stockholm Instagram: theparkco

Face of the Space:

Hanna Melander is The Park's general manager. She started working at an early age and is a believer in learning by doing. She previously worked for several years for a large Scandinavian conference group in movie distribution, marketing/PR and events. She enjoys the dynamic coworking environment and loves witnessing the new startup innovations as they emerge.

erts

In partnership with:

Jonas Almeling
/ Business Sweden

Head of Innovation and Ecosystems

Transitioning from a startup to a scaleup is incredibly exciting. It means you've validated your product in a market and shown consistent growth. But it also means facing a new set of challenges, especially if you want to grow internationally. Jonas Almeling, head of Innovations and Ecosystems at Business Sweden, works mostly with Swedish growth companies and scaleups to access new markets, and he has some advice for those trying to go global.

"Companies from different industries have different challenges, of course," says Jonas, "but what it boils down to is understanding the business culture and communication style in the markets you want to go to." That's where Business Sweden's offices in more than fifty cities around the world come in handy. At its core, the organization is about connecting later stage companies to key local stakeholders and offering tailored consultancy services, such as support in handling cultural differences and understanding regulations in a specific market, so Swedish companies can grow internationally. "We work with companies all over Sweden and in nearly all markets around the world," says Jonas.

If your company has found a product-market fit and you're looking to expand your footprint around the globe, it's important to remember that time is of the essence. "When you analyze the market and your business to see where the best opportunities in the world are, it's crucial to keep in mind that this information is relevant for a limited amount of time," he says. "If you do your research now and then wait twelve months to take action on it, it'll be old, so understanding *when* to do a market analysis for your business is key." Part of that analysis involves doing your due diligence on the market and answering questions like how much time it will take and how much it will cost. Not only will this kind of information be helpful for your own team, it will likely be requested by your investors too.

For Swedish growth-stage companies who are looking to foray into new markets but don't know how to proceed, the Business Sweden Going Global program can help improve your chances with its services tailored to the needs of different kinds of companies. The Leap Accelerator, for instance, is a free applications-based program that helps you build a customized plan and strategy for international expansion through data, on-the-ground insights

Most important tips for startups:

- Learn about the customs and culture of the market
  you want to expand to.
  In order to connect to the customers and consumers
  in a specific market, you first need to understand their
  culture and communication style.

- Perform a market analysis and do your due
  diligence in a market in a timely manner.
  Don't forget that an analysis you do now might
  be irrelevant in a year's time.

- No matter which market you decide to enter,
  building trustworthy relationships is always
  important to business success.
  Nurture existing relationships and broaden
  your network through your existing contacts.

and hands-on coaching. "It helps companies identify which markets to go to and evaluate how much time and resources it'll take to go there, and it helps facilitate relationships in those ecosystems," says Jonas. The accelerator program runs in batches whenever there's a group (of five to ten companies) ready to go, and it accepts around one hundred companies each year.

Then there's the Business Sweden Catalyst program targeted to those that are ready to take action on their expansion plan. "Here, scaleups can apply to receive full funding for their market-entry project," he says. To be considered, growth-stage companies need to apply through the website and, if selected, it involves pitching in front of an investment committee, which decides whether a company receives funding.

The final piece of advice Jonas has for entrepreneurs trying to scale successfully is that good relationships are good for business. Even though it's something we've all heard before, it's still worth reiterating. "No matter what kind of product or service you have, trustworthy relationships are valuable for every kind of company," he says. "So when you go into new markets, be sure to take the time to nurture relationships, reach out to people for that cup of coffee, and tap into existing contacts to broaden your network, whether it's through Business Sweden or Startup Guide or otherwise."

About

Business Sweden's purpose is to help Swedish companies grow global sales and help international companies invest and expand in Sweden. For Swedish companies, it provides strategic advice, sales execution and operational support to help them grow their international revenues. For international companies, it ensures that they can depend on Business Sweden's knowledge, experience and extensive network to identify new business opportunities and achieve an accelerated return on investment.

[Contact]   Email: info@business-sweden.se

[Links]   Web: business-sweden.se/en Facebook: BusinessSweden Twitter: @BusinessSweden

*"When you analyze
the market and your
business to see where
the best opportunities
in the world are,
it's crucial to keep
in mind that this
information is relevant
for a limited amount
of time."*

Natanael Sijanta
/ Daimler AG | me Convention

Director, Global Marketing Communications, Mercedes-Benz Cars

For entrepreneurs, opportunities to network and to learn from people in other industries aren't always readily available or apparent. And yet this is so important, according to Natanael Sijanta, a marketing communications expert who has worked at Daimler, the parent company of Mercedes-Benz, for over twenty years in areas such as branding, sales and management. Natanael knows a thing or two about the value of networking and connecting corporates with startups, and for this reason he's taken a lead role in the development of a unique conference which takes place in Stockholm in 2018. "We noticed a few years ago that there was something missing at the conventions we went to," Natanael says. And looking to fill this gap is how the me Convention – a collaboration between Mercedes-Benz and the annual American media, music and film festival South by Southwest – was born.

"We love what they do at South by Southwest and wanted to bring their open-mindedness to Europe in the form of a conference," says Natanael. The very first me Convention took place in 2017 in Frankfurt. Earlier this year, the me Convention cohosted an event with South by Southwest in Austin, Texas. Stockholm was chosen for the 2018 convention because of the city's entrepreneurial spirit and the noteworthy progress the city has made in becoming a major European tech hub.

One of the key themes addressed by the festival is how leadership models and styles in the workplace are changing dramatically. "Ten years ago," says Natanael, "career paths were predictable, and entrepreneurship wasn't as widespread as it is today." That's why now it's so important for people of various ages and from different sectors to get in touch, he says, adding that rather than try to face the journey all alone, founders should take learning from and exchanging ideas with others seriously.

But this isn't always easy. "Unlike at a big company, where networking opportunities are abundant, people at smaller startups need to make more of an effort to connect with others," he says. On the upside, since corporates are more than willing to discover new ways of thinking, they're keen on working with startups. For example, as part of Daimler's goal to play a major role in shaping mobility of the future, it recently made a significant investment in flying taxi

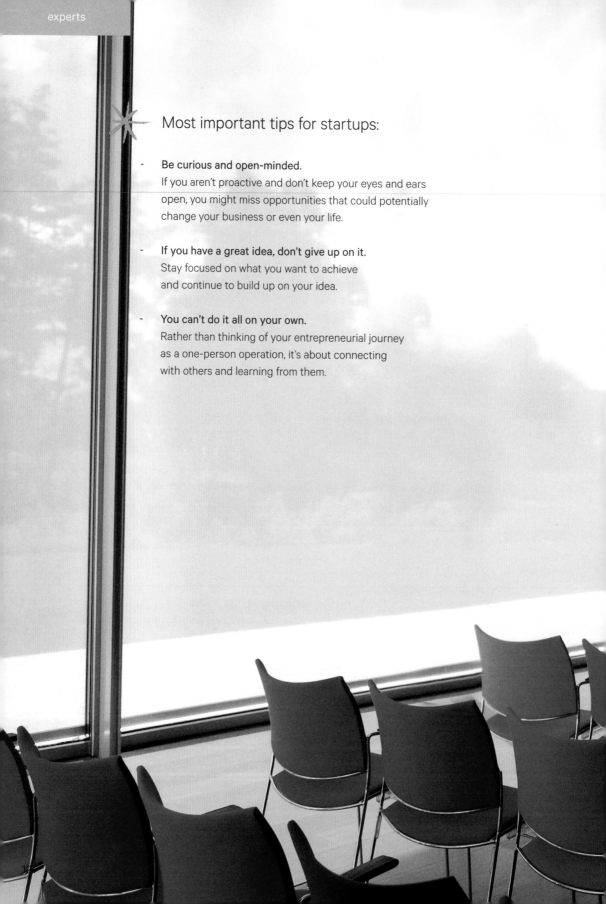

Most important tips for startups:

- **Be curious and open-minded.**
  If you aren't proactive and don't keep your eyes and ears
  open, you might miss opportunities that could potentially
  change your business or even your life.

- **If you have a great idea, don't give up on it.**
  Stay focused on what you want to achieve
  and continue to build up on your idea.

- **You can't do it all on your own.**
  Rather than thinking of your entrepreneurial journey
  as a one-person operation, it's about connecting
  with others and learning from them.

startup Volocopter.

Another thing Natanael considers crucial when it comes to building a company from the ground up is to be receptive to the things happening around you, as this can change your business for the better. One of the me Convention's highlights is a lineup of speakers from all over the world – including from cities such as Sofia (Bulgaria), Almaty (Kazakhstan) and Belfast (UK) – who will share how their respective ecosystems are supporting startups. "These stories are useful not only for people thinking of starting a business," he says, "but also for founders considering expanding or relocating. The cities the speakers launched their business in have a favorable economic environment, an abundance of universities and a promising startup scene." And though these cities aren't the ones people first tend to think of when it comes to tech hubs, they stand out since they're actively bringing about change and trying to create a community that consists of everything from VCs and corporates to accelerators and incubators.

Attendees at the me Convention will also have the chance to participate in mentoring sessions with the speakers and to ask them for insights and advice on the ups and downs of entrepreneurship. A convention of this nature is, as Natanael says, "a must for startups," not only for its networking opportunities but also in how it can inspire entrepreneurs and possibly even influence their business and their thinking.

About

The me Convention (second edition) takes place in Stockholm and is one among many of Daimler's initiatives to get involved with the worldwide startup scene. A cross between a festival and a conference, the me Convention's main aim is to connect inquisitive minds across all industries, including tech, art and design, and to discuss what the future could look like.

[Contact]   Email: natanael.sijanta@daimler.com

[Links]   Web: me-convention.com Facebook: @meconvention Instagram: @meconvention

"If you want to grow, come up with new ideas and be able to collaborate with others, you have to network and be open-minded."

Agnes Malm, Viktoria Källsäter and Jonas Wannelöf / Danske Bank

Growth and Impact Lead SE, Relationship Managers

Growing fast and scaling a startup globally isn't easy. "Setting up internationally takes a lot of time, effort and resources – and time, of course, is one of the scarcest resources for entrepreneurs," says Agnes Malm, growth and impact lead SE at Danske Bank. "There can be a lot of costly mistakes for startups setting up a business in parts of the world where they don't understand the cultural differences and what it means to do business in a country."

That's why Agnes, alongside Danske Bank relationship managers Viktoria Källsäter and Jonas Wannelöf, are working towards making the bank a strategic financial partner for startups and scale-ups – namely, by helping the startups build a network and supporting their growth journey. "Banks, in general, haven't always been good at understanding what startups need," Agnes says, "but we're seeing more and more that there are so many things we can help them out with to go from startup to scale-up,"

Scaling a startup globally is always a tricky process, and there's no set formula for doing it. It can be challenging to find team members and partners in a new market who align with your vision. Not only that, while fast growth is important when it comes to competition and to proving yourself to investors, growing too rapidly without the right people and structures in place typically leads to growth that isn't sustainable. The danger of moving too quickly without a strategy is that it can lead to dire legal and cultural issues down the line.

So how can startup teams with big dreams avoid expensive repercussions and burnout while seeking expansion abroad? "It's important to look for partners and ask for help, so you can focus your time and resources on the most important parts of driving your business forward," says Agnes. Recently, Danske Bank teamed up with nHack Ventures, a program with headquarters in Shanghai. It aims to accelerate the growth of Nordic startup businesses in Asia by offering access to Chinese consumer markets and assisting with prototyping, sourcing, production and local sales as well as raising capital in Asia.

Most important tips for startups:

Ask for help and look for partners.
Setting up internationally takes a lot of time, effort and resources. One way to accelerate this process is to find people, partners and institutions that have solutions to help you grow.

Dare to dream big and have a global mindset from day one.
Set up structures from the very beginning that allow your startup to scale on both a national and international level.

Find the right people to join your growth journey.
It's not always easy to find the right people and partners, but having people along on the ride who align with your vision will make the journey much smoother.

Another initiative, dubbed Danske Bank Growth, supports entrepreneurs at various stages of their journey with a cross-Nordic team of startup-growth advisors who are passionate about helping startups accelerate their growth. They know that running a startup is different from running a traditional company. "When you have global ambitions, you need to focus on running your business rather than spending time on banking and accounts," says Agnes. "If you're starting up, Danske Bank Growth offers fast and easy banking, so you can focus on the things that matter. And as your business scales and becomes more complex, it also provides tailored solutions for companies, and we can set up a team of experts who can help you figure out what your next step is."

Additionally, entrepreneurs in Sweden, Denmark, Norway and Finland can also use The Hub (thehub.se), a free, digital-community platform for growth startups run by Danske Bank and Rainmaking. With almost one thousand startup profiles in Sweden, the platform offers an overview of the startup scene in the country as well as the overall region, and it includes best practices, tools, events and insights on starting up. It also connects startups to talent and investors.

For those who live in Stockholm and want to speak to someone face-to-face about banking or any of these initiatives, Danske Bank holds office hours at SUP46 once every two weeks. "We have a serious interest in helping startups grow," says Agnes. "As a financial institution, we want to step up, be present in society and take this responsibility seriously."

About

Danske Bank is a Nordic bank with strong local roots and bridges to the rest of the world. For more than 145 years, it has helped people and businesses in the Nordics realize their ambitions. It serves personal, business and institutional customers, offering banking services, life insurance and pension, mortgage credit, wealth management, and real estate and leasing services.

[Contact]   Email: **nordicgrowth@danskebank.com**

" It's important to look for partners and ask for help, so you can focus your time and resources on the most important parts of driving your business forward. "

Ted Persson
/ EQT Ventures

Operating Partner

While venture capital is not something all entrepreneurs are keen on getting their hands on, for some, it's a perfectly feasible option. Ted Persson, operating partner at EQT Ventures, acknowledges that, for those beginning their startup journey and in search of a VC, there are challenges that can cost a lot of time and effort. But one way newbies can tackle the daunting task of finding an initial round of funding, he says, is by honing in on a handful of the VCs and angel investors you really want to approach.

If you're ambitious and your company is driven by tech, the VCs he partners with could come in handy. Even when Ted joined EQT Ventures and helped to get it off the ground three years ago, he was no newcomer to the digital space. Since the 1990s, he's founded three digital agencies, ran an incubator, dabbled in social networking, and advised some of the world's leading startups. Nowadays he specializes in product design, user experience, storytelling and branding for startups deeply rooted in technology.

Even though EQT Ventures offers financing, it's actually a hybrid between a VC and a startup. The two dozen people on its team "are not your typical financial investment managers," Ted explains. Rather, they're former entrepreneurs and ex-operators, and as such they can give actionable advice and relevant support. The investment company stands out as one among very few of its kind worldwide, since its team is composed not solely of money experts but of founders who have also gone through the ins and outs of launching a startup. Some are even working on an internal startup called Motherbrain, which keeps them up to speed with the latest methodologies.

Since the partners bring a wealth of knowledge with them in everything from HR to game design and international expansion, this can be beneficial for entrepreneurs specifically seeking support in these areas, no matter where they are in their journey. Ted's team consists of everything from engineers to data scientists, some of whom had a hand in creating well-known tech companies such as Uber and Spotify.

Most important tips for startups:

- Narrow it down to a handful or two of investors you want to approach.
  Be focused when it comes to the investors you aim to meet rather than getting in touch with hundreds of them.

- Be picky when choosing your team members.
  Surround yourself with the right people. This is important as founding a company is a team sport and you can't go at it alone.

- Start and see how far you get.
  It sounds like a cliché but instead of thinking about your idea, simply get started and talk to as many people as possible about it. You're likely to get valuable feedback.

Since EQT Venture's inception in 2016, it has already made a positive impact on around thirty companies. One in particular is a Finnish games developer called Small Giant Game, which EQT Ventures has supported on a hands-on level and which is now quickly growing on a global scale.

Another tip Ted emphasizes for founders, in addition to having a narrow focus when it comes to choosing the VC that's right for you, is going in with the mindset that it's a team sport. "Be diligent about the people you choose to have around you," he says, "because you can't do it on your own." With this in mind, one of the VC's newest initiatives is EQT Access, a program geared toward connecting its startups with its enterprises. The program unlocks opportunities by putting entrepreneurs in touch with advisors and CEOs who belong to EQT Venture's larger companies.

Ultimately, it comes down to taking the bull by the horns to begin with. In the early stages of the entrepreneurial journey, people tend to refrain from talking about their idea and may waste time thinking about it or making sketches, but "you should just get going and see where it takes you," says Ted. Whether you're in the beginning of your journey, have scaled up or are in a stage of growth, "people with loads of experience under their belt who have built up some of the world's biggest tech companies can help you with whatever you need."

About
EQT Ventures invests in tech-driven companies across a range of industries globally with a European focus. As the venture capital arm of Swedish private equity group EQT Partners established in 1994, EQT Ventures launched in 2016. Since then it has supported roughly thirty startups throughout their entrepreneurial journey.

[Contact]   Email: **ted@eqtventures.com**

[Links]   Web: **eqtventures.com** Facebook: **EQT-Ventures-1360176604060711** Twitter: **@eqtventures**

"*Founding a company is a team sport; be diligent about the people you choose to have around you.*"

Didrik Fjeldstad
/ SAS

Vice President Brand and Marketing

Breaking into the travel industry is tough for a startup – not only is it a competitive market, it's also incredibly consolidated – but that doesn't mean you shouldn't try, because there's still plenty of room for improvement and innovation.

Didrik Fjeldstad, vice president of Brand and Marketing at SAS (also known as Scandinavian Airlines) believes there are three key areas in the travel sector that can be improved. "First, more and more people are using mobile devices to book their trips as well as at various points during their journey, so mobile travel is a big one," he says. "There are currently many sources and platforms, and it somehow needs to all be aggregated. Second, since we're now flooded with information from everywhere, curated travel tips and personalized content will become increasingly valuable. Third, disrupting the area of digital payments. At SAS, we work actively within all these areas, and we welcome input and collaborations from the entrepreneurial world to support us in seeking new, innovative solutions."

Having worked with SAS for more than two years, Didrik has seen a plethora of travel services in all shapes and sizes, both digital and physical. He says one of the biggest mistakes that an entrepreneur can make when trying to enter the industry is to be too generic with their product, especially in an industry that's quite mature and has so many players. One way to differentiate your company from others is to put the customer first, which is something that's been important to SAS from the very beginning. "Focusing on the entire customer journey is an absolute must when you're trying to build a business in the travel industry," explains Didrik. At its core, this means creating a top-notch experience for the customer, spanning from the digital experience of planning the trip through to the end of their physical journey.

Drawing from SAS's long-standing customer-centric culture, Didrik offers some tips on how to better serve and understand customers in the travel sector. "Putting data at the center of your customer journey is crucial," he says. "Related to that is knowing your customer's DNA from day one in order to build an IT architecture around it. This way, you have one way of looking at the customer across all your services and, in turn, provide greater relevance and value in the services you offer. Handling personal data is also key, and the best way to gain

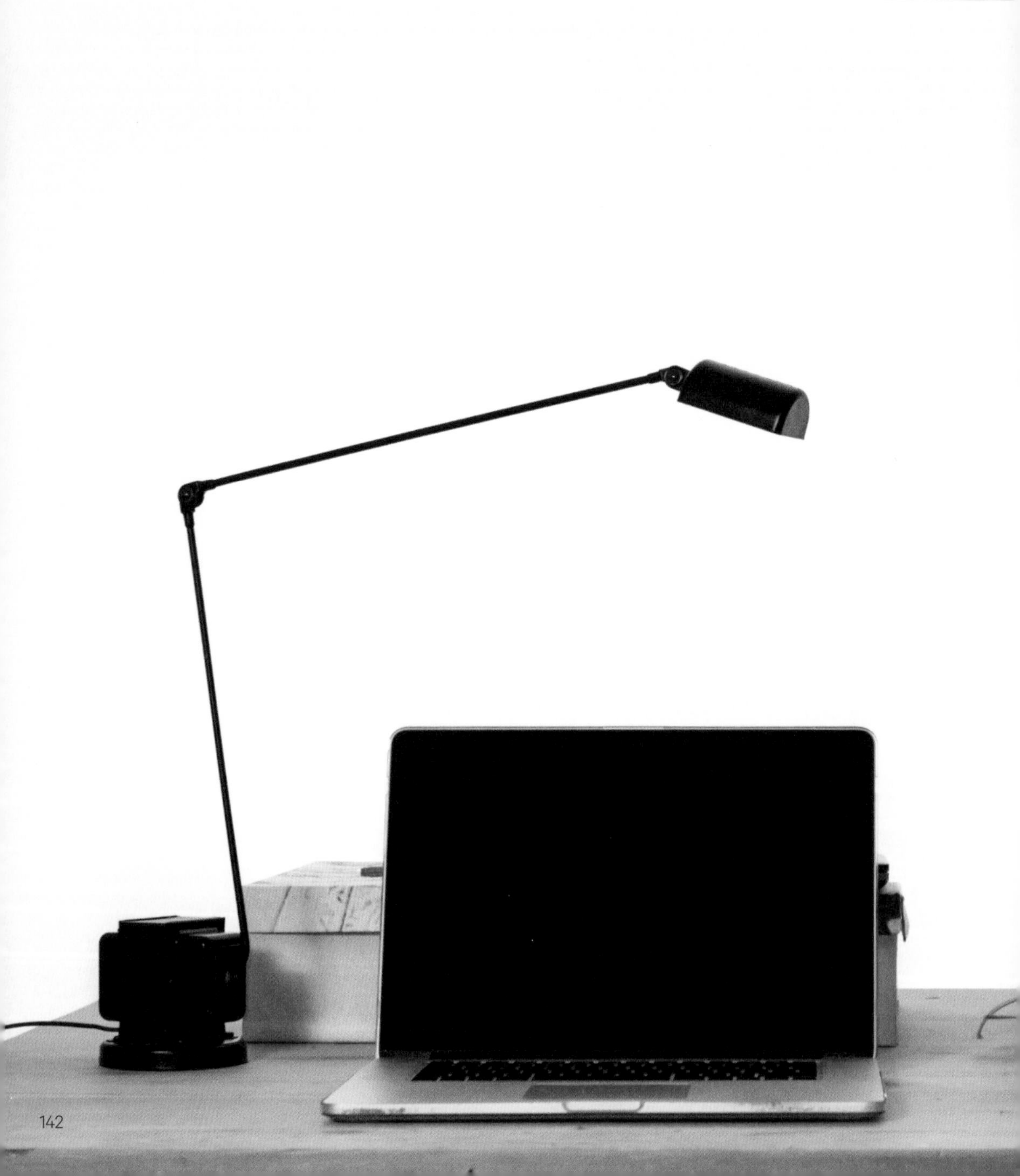

Most important tips for startups:

- The travel industry is a mature and competitive sector; don't be too generic with your product or service.
Research the field you'd like to innovate within, and make sure you're offering something that will add value to the customer experience as a whole.

- Focus on the customer, always.
It's important to understand your customers and the reasons they want to travel to better serve their needs. You can start by putting data at the center of your customer journey.

- Don't be afraid to test things out while prototyping.
Go out to an airport or hotel and talk to people. Ask them to try out your product or service and provide feedback, if possible. It'll be incredibly insightful.

consent is to use data with caution and with unconditional focus on creating value for the consumer. Also, don't be shy about going out to the airport and hotel with prototypes; it can be immensely insightful. Lastly, understand the emotional drivers of your customers."
The final point emphasizes the importance of learning about the many different reasons people travel, because this will help you develop a more relevant and impactful product or service for a modern traveler.

SAS realizes how hard it can be to gain a foothold in the travel industry, so they started SAS Labs (labs.sas), a program where entrepreneurs and startups from all over the world team up with SAS to explore and co-develop ideas and technologies to propel the travel industry forward. Unlike typical programs for startups, SAS Labs doesn't have an application deadline. Instead, it works on an open rolling basis, supporting entrepreneurs who'd like to focus on the specific tracks in which SAS would like to innovate, such as service optimization, connected experiences and sustainability. In relation to the sustainability track, Didrik says, "One of the only requirements is that we want these startups to contribute to a positive environmental or social impact within the travel sector."

Additionally, there's the SAS Scholarship program (https://scandinaviantraveler.com/en/sasscholarship) for entrepreneurs with an idea that aims to reshape the travel industry. Three winners receive a prize that includes a trip to a destination that's related to their idea within SAS's global network as well as access to mentors who can help them further develop their concept.

About
Aviation is a vital part of Scandinavian infrastructure. SAS maintains the highest frequency of departures to and from Scandinavia and connects smaller regional airports with larger hubs. Its vision is to make life easier for Scandinavia´s frequent travelers. With SAS, customers become part of a community experiencing easy, joyful and reliable services, delivered the Scandinavian way. SAS is headquartered in Stockholm and has subsidiaries all over Scandinavia.

"Focusing on the entire customer journey is an absolute must when you're trying to build a business in the travel industry."

ders

Amir Marandi

CEO / Zaver

Amir Marandi, an Iranian-Swedish entrepreneur, was born in Tehran and moved to Stockholm with his parents when he was only six years old. While studying for his master's degree in Sweden, he noticed that his fellow students were were buying and selling books, gadgets and even cars from one another, but they didn't have good options for transferring the cash for the goods. Observing this, he saw an opportunity to improve the peer-to-peer payment experience. Together with a classmate, Linus Malmén, Marandi decided to build an app called Zaver that would give buyers more choices in how they paid for books or gadgets, and give sellers more assurance that they would get paid.

What did you study in school?
I was at KTH Royal Institute of Technology, studying mechanical engineering for a bachelor's degree. Then I started my master of science in industry of management, but I jumped off because we started Zaver.

Did you have other jobs before Zaver?
I worked at Nordnet Bank during my studies, in product development. I got involved in the finance industry by working there.

How did you get the idea for Zaver?
As a student, you end up buying or selling stuff through classifieds. Everything from cars to iPhones change hands every day. Let's say you want to buy a car or a phone. You find someone through a classified ad, and you meet up. The most fragile part is the payment process: the seller wants the money in his or her bank account, and the buyer wants a plan or to pay by installments. This is doable – it exists in e-commerce – but for peer to peer, this was not an option. Especially for transactions with higher prices on them, there weren't payment options available for peer to peer. The only thing available was bank transfers.

We solve that because we pay the seller directly to their bank account, and the buyer can choose what method they want to pay with through our app. Let's say they pay through installments. The buyer can drive the car home, and the seller knows they will get the money from us. If they don't have payment options, people don't buy from their peers; they'll go to car dealerships or buy phones via e-commerce sites, where these kinds of payment methods are available.

How did you get off the ground?

Starting a FinTech company and payment service isn't the easiest, because you need to have a lot of tech platforms, plus permissions from the Financial Supervisory Authority. Our early struggles were that we needed funding, permissions, and experienced people on the board who know how to get those permissions. We also needed a lot of platforms, like transaction surveillance and back-office software. We developed the transaction surveillance app and the admin panel ourselves, and then we also found service providers. This was fairly rough. Maybe it's not meant for some students to launch a payment service.

What was your strategy for getting things done early on?

We used our engineering framework for solving problems: We took one problem at a time, and we prioritized different problems. We started with the hardest and went down the list. We'd focus, let's say, on funding, and then on permissions, and then on something else. I think that a lot of startups don't understand the potential in a team; as a team, you can achieve much more than as individuals.

By doing one thing at a time, we were able to contact the right investors and get the right permissions from the Swedish FSA, even though we were young and not that experienced in the financial industry. We bootstrapped through every struggle, and once we had great people around us, like investors and others who believed in us, it was easier to get the confidence we needed.

A lot of problems aren't being solved because people don't think they can solve them. But people are smarter than they think they are.

What's your day like as CEO?

My job is to make sure that we as a team fulfill our obligations to ourselves and reach our objectives, everything from product development to human resources. But we're a small startup where everyone is involved in the daily work. Right now, we're three employees.

How have you accomplished so much with a small team?

When you're at a smaller size, you can make quick decisions. We saw this opportunity to improve this industry, and one of our core goals is to create a payment service with new modern technology and to automate this process. We wanted to reduce everything we could that was manual work. Banks have a lot of back office staff, and we didn't want to become like that, so we focused on building a platform where the machines can – as far as they are able – make the decisions.

"You need to move forward fast. You don't have time for over-calculating. Moving fast is what makes you different from the large organizations you're going to compete with."

How did you raise the funds you needed?

We did it in two rounds. We didn't look for funding from VC. We went to entrepreneurs, and I think that was also one of the best decisions we made.

The first investor to believe in Zaver was Bo Mattson, the founder of Cint. After that, we could contact other potential investors who showed interest. One of the most important parts in raising money for us was getting the right investors. If you don't get the right ones, you'll meet a lot of problems, so we focused on our strategy for funders, finding ex-entrepreneurs who had gone through this journey before, or current entrepreneurs who were going through it in the present, and who knew exactly how it is to start a startup from the beginning.

What was the moment you thought, "I can really do this"?

The first transaction. Some people say that you'll be as happy as you can be when you have your first child. I can only say that it was the closest feeling to that. That transaction was nothing special in terms of revenue, but we'd worked so hard, for so many months, to show and prove that what we're doing will be used. We knew that the first user to use Zaver would be the beginning of this journey. When that happened, it felt like we'd succeeded, even if it was just the beginning of this.

What was the transaction?

It was someone renting out their apartment, so they used Zaver to collect the rent. The renter could pay at the end of the month, but the owner could get the money in bank account at beginning of month. That was actually surprising to us as a way to use Zaver.

How does Zaver make money?

Today, we're completely free to the sellers – the payment receivers. We make money through interest when someone chooses to set up a payment plan by installments. Due to the automation of our processes, we have individualized interest that correlates to your creditworthiness. The system automatically chooses an interest rate for you.

How do buyers and sellers find you?

We haven't marketed much yet, but we will soon. What we've done so far is take Zaver onto social media. We have some ads on Facebook and Google, and we collaborate with some Facebook groups.

Most importantly, we see that we're starting to get some of the word-of-mouth effect of the product. When someone buys something with us and they feel satisfied, they use us to sell something to someone else. And then so on.

What do you think was your biggest mistake?

Our biggest mistake was at the beginning, when we tried to satisfy everyone in every decision. We weren't experienced, and we thought that making everyone happy would create a better culture, but it doesn't; it creates a false one. We always ended up with compromises, and that is not the best idea.

What do you like about being an entrepreneur in Stockholm?

Stockholm is one of the best cities to found a startup in, because people care about what you're doing and not who you are. If you have a good idea and a great team, you'll get the funding you need. There are lot of early adopters here who want to test new products. It feels like society is near the digital world in that they'll support the startups' products. There are great and smart people working here, which is also an asset.

What's your big goal for Zaver?

The goal is to prove this concept here in Sweden. Then, we want to expand to different countries and solve a real problem for everyone. And we've seen that so far at last, our product does so. Maybe in the future we'll be able to connect different countries where you could use the same payment service and still get all the different payment options. We want people to feel secure buying across borders.

What advice would you give to startup founders?

As an early stage company, it's better to make ten quick decisions where eight turn out to be good, instead of making only three excellent decisions. That's because you need to move forward fast. You don't have time for over-calculating. Moving fast is what makes you different from the large organizations you're going to compete with.

[About]   Zaver is a peer-to-peer payment processing platform that offers options such as credit and pay-over-time to buyers, and also reduces fraud risk for sellers, making it possible for people to purchase big-ticket items such as cars and phones from each other.

[Links]   Web: zaver.se Facebook: zaverSE

What are your top work essentials?
Laptop, Slack, and Gmail.

At what age did you found your company?
Twenty-one.

What's your most-used app?
Gmail.

**What's the most valuable piece of advice
you've been given?**
Find people who are smarter than you in their own fields.

What's your greatest skill?
Connecting dots. Seeing the whole picture
even if it's not obvious.

Elsa Bernadotte

COO and Cofounder / Karma

Elsa Bernadotte is a shining example of what happens when genuine entrepreneurial spirit combines with the supportive and diverse business culture of Stockholm's startup scene. As the founder of Karma, a startup that is successfully fighting food waste, Elsa possesses a rare insight for business as well as for identifying new ways to help individuals and the world at large.

Tell us a little bit about the early days when you founded Karma.
Karma is actually my second venture. Prior to Karma, I founded Pop Fruits, a healthy ice-cream alternative made of frozen fruit on sticks, where I spearheaded operations in four different geographical markets. This included the business development, setting up production in southern Vietnam and the sales and marketing operations. I eventually sold the company and soon thereafter founded Karma together with my current cofounders Hjalmar, Ludvig and Mattis.

Initially, we started the company as a platform where users could upload deals they uncovered for a range of different products and share them with an online community. This data was helpful to both retailers who wanted to make better offerings and to consumers who were seeking better deals. When we launched the early versions of the platform, however, our users didn't behave as we'd anticipated, and that's what eventually led to our pivot in 2016.

Was it difficult to make this pivot?
It really was a learning process, and a necessary one for doing the work we do now. Nine months in, people loved uploading discounts for everything to the platform – food, clothing, movies, all of it was being shared – and we were gaining huge amounts of crowd-sourced data on products and deals. This was where the difficulties started. The target groups varied wildly, and we were struggling to keep the offerings niched and relevant enough to attract the same target audience. We had to face the hard fact that we'd have to consolidate our efforts in order to remain effective at what we were doing, so we started looking at which data sets had the most value and where we had the most traction. What we discovered was a massive number of restaurants trying to find customers for excess food. It was then that we realized the problem we were meant to solve: food waste. There was a huge market, and no one was trying to solve it at scale. From further research, we also found that global food waste amounts to a staggering total cost of a trillion dollars per year.

What was your biggest mistake during this founding period where you were figuring out and implementing your new approach?

To be honest, we made many mistakes in the early days, especially in the first few months; but for each mistake made, a new opportunity was understood. For example, we didn't embrace MVP-thinking as much as we could have. Instead, we tried to build something that would scale and attract a mass market from day one, which ultimately slowed us down. And we didn't stress-test our theories enough or work with an end user – but now we do. These and other processes changed as we went. Through working very hard and making many, many mistakes, we've learned to get into the habit of speed in all that we do, to test and measure literally everything, and to become super customer-obsessed. In our view, it's best to strive for perfection. Even if we don't reach it 100 percent, we're most effective as a company when there's an ideal scenario to envision and aim for.

Is there a decision you made during this time that you think was a particularly good one as you learned more?

The best decision was making the pivot from a deals platform to focusing on food waste. Then, after tackling restaurants, the best decision we made was to also get involved with grocery stores. Fairly early on, grocery stores reached out about the same problem that restaurants had: excess food. This was a big deal for us at the time, because Karma was initially only available for cafes, restaurants and bakeries. Then, the biggest grocery store in Sweden approached us. We were very cautious with that decision, because we didn't want to end up where we'd started off by diluting the platform and not addressing a specific user group. We decided we could do it, but in a controlled way, starting with just a couple of stores in order to get some iterative cycles going. For that, we took on ready-made meals that the grocery stores were making. Now we have an exclusive contract with 90 percent of the grocery market. With groceries now being the fastest-growing category in the platform, this was absolutely the right decision.

"We feel the most purpose when we connect with a process or product that makes a difference in people's lives."

Are there things you would've done differently?

Certainly, but it's also the case that working through less-than-ideal decisions was how we eventually uncovered the most important things we now know to work so well. We had to work and learn. Early on, for example, we thought we were data-driven; but even so, we were not yet data-informed. Gathering data versus identifying its best possible uses are two very different things. When it came to product, we should've just gone out and done small data-driven tests instead of at times following a feeling or an opinion. Lessons like these are where we truly came to appreciate how working hard means nothing if you're not working smart. Trying to do certain things manually, for example, only reinforced our understanding of how important it is to discover what can feasibly be automated or digitized. Perhaps most important of all, we now know that everything takes twice as long as you think, so we set short deadlines to get into the habit of speed. If we set long deadlines, it will still take twice as long anyway.

What other processes have changed?

Testing things early and often has become a thing of major importance to us, from our product to our internal processes. We focus a lot more now on doing things that don't scale, in order to learn what should and shouldn't be built at scale. It's always better, in my opinion, to anticipate and enjoy the process of trial and error rather than let it – or any other change in plans based on new information – surprise you. All of our changes have also taught me to embrace change as part of a learning process and not to compromise on working with something that I truly love – something that is solving a real problem. All of us here love being entrepreneurs, and we feel the most purpose when we connect with a process or product that makes a difference in people's lives.

What advice would you give to other professionals?

The best things I can suggest are to always start sooner, since there's always more work to be done than anyone expects, and everything takes a little bit longer than imagined. Also, test everything. Building products alongside the people and businesses you're trying to serve makes things much better later on when you're working at scale. It's always better to solve a problem earlier rather than later. Next, test things quickly. Though it's important to be methodical, at the end of the day, an MVP mindset is key. No amount of thoughtful research and testing is of any use if it takes too much time to help your business face its current challenges. By having an MVP mindset in everything you do, you're constantly focusing on the most important sources of value that you offer and can deliver on. Lastly, when it comes to your own capabilities, don't underestimate yourself or overestimate others.

In addition to what you like about your work, what do you like about working in your city?
I truly love it here. Stockholm has a great ecosystem for startups, especially tech startups.
We have a lot of great access to incubators and coworking spaces, as well as lots of tech-savvy,
curious and highly educated people who want to test new things. The city is also very central
and has a lot of events and networks for finding new hires and investors. We have active role
models and investors who you can definitely meet if you have the ability to fight a little bit for
it. Many people make themselves available to offer advice, offer "dos and don'ts," and will bring
you into the networks of their peers. This makes Stockholm accessible as both a business
cluster and more generally as a community. Financially, there's also a lot of local capital from
successful entrepreneurs and investors for those who need funding. I'm also a big fan of many
of the local podcasts. I guess I would say that it's not just one thing that makes Stockholm a
great city, but a combination of things that drive this ecosystem and make it stronger each year.
For me, it's been a huge change over the last five years when I started off – a good change.

[About]   Karma is a marketplace that enables restaurants and grocery stores to reduce food waste
by selling unsold food at a discount direct to consumers. Sellers are able to generate
revenue from food that would otherwise go to waste, reach new customers and reduce their
environmental impact, while users get delicious food at half-price or lower.

[Links]   Web: **karma.life** Facebook: **elsa.bernadotte** Twitter: **@YourKarmaApp**

What are your top work essentials?
iPad and Apple pencil. Then MacBook, iPhone
and Bose noise-cancelling headphones.

At what age did you found your first company?
Twenty-four.

What's your most-used app?
Evernote.

**What's the most valuable piece of advice
you've been given?**
To get comfortable being uncomfortable
and embrace a growth mindset.

What's your greatest skill?
Adaptability and being a quick learner.

Imad Elabdala

Founder and Chief Executive Officer / Kidnovation

A civil war can derail so many people's lives, but not Imad Elabdala's. He found the strength
to turn very bad news into a will to do better. Imad is a social entrepreneur from Syria.
With his engineer mentality and his passion for art and storytelling, he has transformed
his traumatic experience into the drive to try and solve a huge worldwide problem:
the psychological issues of refugee children.

Where are you from?

I was born in 1984 in Damascus, but I grew up and lived in Homs, the third-largest city in Syria.
In 2008, I got my bachelor's degree in materials engineering in Yerevan, Armenia. I then studied
my master's in Homs, Syria, and started my entrepreneurial career, founding an engineering
company.

But in 2011, the civil war broke out and took everything from me: my company and many of my
friends and family members. I saw people, including friends, killed on the street. Nobody was
saying anything. No foreign journalists were allowed in Syria. I felt I was forced to do something.

What did you do?

I took it upon myself to report on what was going on. As I was able to speak English, I contacted
the US television news channel CNN, and I started making videos for them – and also for the
British BBC and the Arabic Al Jazeera – as an activist reporter. I learned how to be a reporter
by doing it.

How long did you work as a war reporter?

For two years. When my city was destroyed, I had to search for a safe space for myself
and my family, which includes my three sisters, one brother and two parents. So we left Syria
and moved to Jordan. There, I helped to get aid for the refugees in the camps; for example,
by distributing medicines for children.

When did you arrive in Sweden?

In 2013. I was able to reach this country the hard way, by smuggling my family through Turkey
and Greece, and then traveling to Northern Europe until we arrived in Stockholm. Sweden was
the first European country to open its doors to Syrian refugees, and we were able to get asylum.

How difficult was it to start a new life?

My family and I are educated and we speak English, so it was not difficult to integrate for work. Understanding Nordic traditions and having a social life was tougher. People here are friendly but not very open. Anyway, I got an engineer job with AGA, the biggest Swedish gas company, and I worked there for one year. Then in 2014 I decided to quit my career and pursue my dream.

Why did you resign from a well-paid job?

I had suffered from post-traumatic stress disorder, and in order to heal I'd studied therapeutic techniques designed to help sufferers of PTSD. It took me more than one year to regain a balance, and then it just hit me: in the world, there are twenty-seven million refugee kids who have had my experience, and only about 5 percent can be helped recover from their trauma by some non-profit organizations. In practice, it is impossible to send a psychologist to every child. This is why I quit. I decided to put my career aside and dedicate myself to creating a solution for making psycho-social support available for them everywhere in the world.

Which idea did you have in mind?

I wanted to make a tool that could be used to give psychological support to refugee children. The tool had to be simple, low cost, scalable and easy to use. As a hobby, I've always loved storytelling. In Syria, I wrote scripts for theatre shows for children. So I figured out that I would embed the best practices of psychology to tackle these problems via stories.

How did you start?

With my savings, I bought an old car, named her "Kate," and then spent 2015 traveling and volunteering at the Red Cross to help my fellow refugees. I also did a lot of research about the best science and best practices to develop a therapy tool for traumatized kids.

In 2016, I returned to Stockholm with my project to found a startup and create my first book: *Sarah's Journey: Dreams Make Any Place Home*. It's the story of an eight-year-old refugee girl hero who is meant to be a role model for displaced children; one who looks like them, shares their experiences and helps them feel positive, self-confident and safe. I wrote it in collaboration with professors of psychology at Stockholm University and University of Vienna, incorporating story-based psychological methods such as cognitive behavioral therapy, exposure therapy and psychodynamic therapy.

" I love working in this tech startup community because Stockholm is a super organized city, but it's not obsessed with competition like Silicon Valley. Here, it's more about collaboration, helping each other among entrepreneurs. "

What were your early struggles, and how did you overcome them while starting up?
I knocked on a lot of doors, but nobody knew me, and so I kept being rejected. There's still
a stigma surrounding refugees and their trustworthiness. Luckily, I found Impact Hub
Stockholm, a community that supports social entrepreneurs. They offered me a discounted
package for a working space. It's where my startup Kidnovation was born.

It was great to be surrounded by like-minded people: other social entrepreneurs who were
willing to do something good. But at that point, I had finished all my savings. So in November
2016, I decided to launch a Kickstarter campaign to finance my book, which was written
in three languages: English, Swedish and Arabic.

Was it a successful campaign?
Yes, It was a successful campaign, but it was less than I expected. The project got 352 backers
who pledged 227,101 SEK out of the 218,000 SEK goal. I did a great job with social media to
spread the word, so I'd expected to reach ten times the goal! It was a big business lesson for
me: even if the idea and the company were strong, the timing was wrong. I had launched the
campaign just before Christmas, when all the charities and non-profit organizations are asking
for donations. People trust what they know, especially big names like the Red Cross; whereas
we were totally new.

Did you ever think of abandoning your project?
No, I didn't. I believed in it. For me, it's a one-way ticket, and there's no way to give up.
I developed the product testing it with children and working with schools. Being an engineer,
I also created an app to measure the impact of the book. I can boast that my startup is one
of the very few social companies with a system that can use data for implementing its project.

How did you move on from the first failure?
Sarah's Journey was supposed to be ready for Christmas 2017, but there were a lot of delays in
production; for example, there were problems with illustrators. Finally, I made my best decision
ever: to not publish the book. Instead, I applied for support from Reach for Change, a non-profit
organization founded in Sweden in 2010. It backs social entrepreneurs with innovations that
solve pressing issues facing children. It helps innovators like me through seed funding as well
as providing access to business expertise and networking opportunities. It's very difficult to be
accepted, and it usually takes two or three years to make it. My project made it on the first try
and was approved in December 2017.

What are your next steps?

The Reach for Change's incubation program lasts three years with the goal of making our business scalable and sustainable. Kidnovation not only received money but it's also going to benefit from the best consultancy in its field, including advice about media communication and PR. My next steps will be hiring a couple of employees, selecting a board of experts and raising the quality level of my products.

I believe I have to focus more on being an artist besides being an engineer. I also learned that in order to deliver quality work, I have to put time aside for the creative work and to completely focus on being an author, and then to put other time aside for being an entrepreneur. Doing both things at the same time was a mistake.

Do you plan to stay in Stockholm?

Yes, I do. I love working in this tech startup community, because Stockholm is a super organized city but it's not obsessed with competition like Silicon Valley. Here, it's more about collaboration, helping each other among entrepreneurs. I only wish I'd spent more time studying the Swedish business mentality before founding my startup. My experience as an entrepreneur in Syria was so different from what I found in Sweden. But, hey, learning by doing is the best way. Making mistakes and falling forward.

Are you totally healed from your war trauma?

I'm still losing family members who remained in Syria. But I try to look at the bright side of life for coping with emotions and stress.

[About]   Kidnovation is the world's first media innovation lab for displaced children. The startup combines scientific research with art and storytelling to reach the hearts and minds of every child who suffered from trauma.

[Links]   Web: kidnovation.se Facebook: Kidnovation Twitter: @Kidnovation_Lab

What are your top work essentials?
Noise-cancelling earbuds.

At what age did you found your company?
I was thirty-two.

What's your most-used app?
The project management application Trello
for team collaboration.

**What's the most valuable piece of advice
you've been given?**
To slow down and look after my health.

What's your greatest skill?
Dare to make mistakes and ask for help.

Joel Hellermark

Founder and CEO / Sana Labs

Joel Hellermark spent most of his childhood living in Asia, from Tokyo to Kuala Lumpur and Singapore. With both of his parents working at IBM, he became interested in problem solving through technology at an early age. By the time he was a senior in high school, he'd already started developing the initial Sana algorithm, which soon grew into a thriving artificial intelligence company focused on improving online education.

How did the idea for Sana Labs come about? Where did it all start?
I have a background in applying machine learning to different prediction and personalization tasks. I saw that the education industry was making a change towards online and realized that all education that's online is going to be completely personalized to how you learn – and it's going to be data driven. I figured someone had to create the engine that would power that shift. That's what we set out to do.

Why the education industry? How did you zero in on that niche?
It's one of the most data-rich industries in the world. As we interact with these platforms, they collect an immense amount of data about how we learn; for example, how long it takes you to answer a certain question. It's an industry which lends itself very well to machine learning. It's also one of the industries where machine learning could have the greatest impact as we make the shift from a one-size-fits-all approach to truly personalized education. Historically, everyone has received the exact same information in the exact same way, and what machine learning has set out to do is to shift that model so every single student receives a completely unique path through a curriculum.

You've been coding since you were a kid and founded your first tech company when you were sixteen. How did you get into that?
My mom and dad both worked at IBM. My mom was a chemist, so she was more in research; and my dad worked in business development. When I was thirteen, I got into some online courses at Stanford where you could teach yourself to program. As a function of that, I got my first assignment as a programmer quite early on, but I think the inspiration was really from my parents, who were bringing leading-edge research to the masses to solve some of the world's most important problems and making it personal and relevant for millions of people.

Where did Sana itself start? You were working on the beta version as a senior in high school, right?

Yeah, exactly. I started researching the algorithms that would allow you to personalize education, and they performed really well. Because of that, I ended up closing the first round of funding in my senior year in high school and then pursued it full-on after graduating.

How much did you raise in that first round?

It was a million dollars total.

What were your peers doing? Is this a high school where everyone graduates with million-dollar projects?

No, not really. It was a leading high school in Sweden, but I think most people were preparing for their college studies. In Sweden, we have this program where if you're studying economics, every student in their third year has to start a company, so I think in general there's an entrepreneurial spirit in the education system here. But my peers were certainly not building companies at that point.

Did something change in the field of AI and machine learning to make what you do possible?

I don't think this would have been possible just ten years back, or five years back. What's really enabled personalized education at this scale is a breakthrough in deep learning: algorithms that can find tendencies and leverage patterns directly from existing data. Historical approaches have relied, to a large degree, upon a lot of human expertise, but now for the first time you can have the system learn by itself. Then you can scale it in a fundamentally new way and uncover much more about the roots and tendencies than has been historically possible. This allows you to see better results. Deep learning really enables personalization at a whole new scale while also improving performance.

What has been the biggest roadblock or the biggest challenge so far?

Most online education players are looking to personalize their experiences. Keeping up with that demand – and scaling the platform and the organization to keep up with that demand – has been a big challenge. We have to reduce the deployment time so we can add everyone who wants to integrate. It's a lot about developing the API so it integrates smoothly into all kinds of educational platforms.

"Look for those problems where new data sets and technology have come to life and where there's a problem that desperately needs to be solved. It's at those inflection points where you build some of the most meaningful companies."

What are some of the platforms that want to use Sana?

The largest market by far is the US, but it's very much global. It's everything ranging from Rosetta Stone, a leading provider of language education, to NE, which is one of Sweden's largest publishers. It's really in a range of applications, from language to mathematics to learning to code.

You recently participated in Duolingo's global AI challenge. How did that turn out?

We won their "global benchmark," where they compared approaches to personalizing education. The challenge was to predict what future mistakes language-learning students would make, based on the mistakes they'd made in the past. We ended up winning every single category on all the evaluation metrics.

Who were you competing with, and what did you have that they didn't?

A few researchers from Cambridge University – some very prominent researchers in the field – and also NYU's Computation and Cognition Lab, and a Chinese company that specializes in language modeling. There were a few others, too. They'd all taken an approach that relied on the main experts in the field, whereas we took an approach that relied on deep learning. Rather than manually finding the rules and the tendencies, we'd developed a system that could uncover them, and that allowed us to uncover more rules and tendencies than a human possibly could. Hence, we were able to surpass the limitations of human expertise.

Have you made any big mistakes while developing Sana Labs?

I think if you're a B2B company, your highest priority should be getting case studies in your first year of existence. In the beginning, just proving the value is the most important aspect. That's one of the key learnings and something that we could have done better. We went for some significant contracts early on, which slowed down getting those first few case studies.

Do you have any other advice for someone trying to start up a company?

I think you should look for inflection points where you find something that's just been made possible and something that's desperately needed. Look for those problems where new data sets and technology have come to life, and where there's a problem that desperately needs to be solved. It's at those inflection points where you build some of the most meaningful companies.

I also like to emphasize ambition in that I think it's almost easier to execute an incredibly ambitious project than a niche-y one, because having an ambitious project allows you to attract the best investors and the best talent. It gets easier to solve the problem.

What's the fundamental problem that you set out to solve, if you could sum it up?
Combining immense datasets that have been made available through online education with deep learning to make personalized education accessible to everyone. That was the inflection point. New datasets becoming available paired with this immense societal need.

Why Stockholm? What made you decide to base the company here?
I think the Stockholm community has really good momentum right now, which has been catalyzed by several unique companies that have been built here. Look at the effects of having Klarna and Spotify. Here in Stockholm, you have a great amount of high-quality talent as well as high-quality investors, which are now looking at which new companies to invest in. So if you're one of these really meaningful companies, you have a great opportunity to attract the best talent and investors.

What are your main goals for Sana labs?
Our ambition is really to achieve ubiquity. If you're learning something online, it should be powered by Sana. Our hope is to empower every single student with a personalized learning experience.

Who are your biggest allies, and who have been your biggest critics?
The education industry is very empirically driven in that you need great proof if you're going to come in and change something, so I think it's really key for a player in that field to build case studies in order to get trust from the community. If you intend to do so, you can do great things; but without proof, I think you have the industry against you. So that's something we focused a lot on: building case studies and proving that the technology makes a meaningful difference.

When it comes to allies, I think people are generally keen to improve education. We've received an immense amount of support from entrepreneurs and investors here in Stockholm, and also different stakeholders in the community. I think if you make sure to build a good case for yourself and your product, the education community is very supportive.

So basically, the industry can be your biggest enemy or your biggest ally.
Exactly. If you want them on your side, you just have to build trust.

[About] Sana Labs is an artificial intelligence company that harnesses the power of machine learning to help online education providers make their content more personalized for each student. Sana Labs' platform gains insights into how people learn by processing huge amounts of data using deep neural networks.

[Links] Web: sanalabs.com Twitter: @sanalabs

What are your top work essentials?
Clara Labs for coordination, nathan.ai for AI/ML
news and Asana for project management.

At what age did you found your company?
Nineteen.

What app do you use the most?
Apple Notes.

**What's the most valuable piece of advice
you've been given?**
Focus.

What's your greatest skill?
Synthesizing.

Sofie Lindblom

CEO and Founder / ideation360

Sofie Lindblom has been around the globe – from San Francisco to Singapore – but eventually she landed back in Stockholm, where she was born and raised. After managing innovation globally at Spotify, she left there and teamed up with Innovation 360 Group to form a new subsidiary – ideation360 – focused on helping organizations design and manage their innovation initiatives.

How did you get involved with ideation360?

Here, I can thank my curiosity. I was scrolling through LinkedIn and saw an interview with Magnus Penker, the founder of the Innovation 360 Group, and I was truly impressed by the framework he'd developed to assess the innovation capabilities of organizations. That's how I started digging into the company and what they were doing. I contacted Magnus, and we got along very well. We shared stories about working with innovation, and then eventually we met and he offered me the role of CEO and cofounder of a company they were just starting: ideation360.

What was that first meeting like?

You know when you meet people and you feel like you get smarter just by talking to them? It was one of those moments. Both Magnus and I had very hectic schedules, but we managed to squeeze in a lunch at Urban Deli in Stockholm – so very central, and very busy. We talked for so long that suddenly I had to run and didn't have time to pay the bill, so Magnus was very nice to pay for the lunch. Afterward, he sent me a very long email about what they wanted to do with ideation360 and Innovation 360 Group to become a global home for innovation.

What prepared you to take on such a huge role?

I was Global Innovation Manager at Spotify, so my background in innovation management and how to make innovation happen in an organization has been incredibly valuable. Of course, it's a tremendous help having Spotify be so successful and having a good reputation when it comes to working with innovation and disrupting the music industry. A lot of examples could be borrowed from how we did things there.

What are some of those things you learned from your time at Spotify?
The key thing here – regardless of whether you are Spotify or Ericsson or a family-owned
company with ten employees – is the leadership and their view on innovation: how important
they think it is, and how much they're willing to invest in it. Daniel Ek is the founder of Spotify
and really has an in-depth understanding of this, and he's always on the lookout for what's
happening in the world. You need an understanding of not only how to adapt and take
opportunities but also how to drive the world in the direction you want it to go.

**Okay, let's back up. How did your childhood and early adult years shape what you're
doing now?**
That's a very good question, and we could make a book out of that alone.

Let's make one paragraph.
I've always been curious. I think that's one of the key ingredients. Growing up in a suburb of
Stockholm was very safe, and the problems I was encountering as a teenager were more typical
teenage problems than anything dramatic. On the other hand, I was a little bit of an underdog:
always quiet, not in the cool gang. I wanted to have good grades and do a good job.
And coming into a different chapter of my life, I realized I could take risks, but do it in
a smart way. That's always been exciting for me. And when you do it once, it's hard to stop.

Do you think there was one moment in your life where you truly became an entrepreneur?
I think the second you quit your job in a big company and go and do your own thing, you
become an entrepreneur, but there's a difference between sleeping in your living room, writing
code as a freelancer and having the ambition of building a global company. A lot of people want
to be entrepreneurs, but it's not very glamorous – at least, not in the beginning.

What are some of the biggest challenges you've faced so far?
I think in the first year, you learn and you do everything for the first time. It makes the second
year easier in many ways, but also new challenges present themselves. And it's exactly like
growing up as a human, right? You learn certain things, but then some things you learned
become irrelevant as you grow bigger or older. Change is the new constant. You have to be
in a constant mode of taking in what's happening around you and having a way of taking action
on it. It's true for individuals and it's true for the companies we work with.

*" I think it's important
to make the mistakes
as early as possible. "*

Who's using ideation360?

We have a very broad spectrum of customers, and how we support those companies is different depending on what their ambition is. We can do something as small as helping them run a hackathon or as large as implementing a fully functional innovation-management system. We have ongoing relationships with our enterprise customers, and we also have a subscription tier where we don't do any kind of coaching or have an in-person relationship, but we support those customers through video conferences and blog posts.

What are your big plans and goals for ideation360?

One is to really help the customers we have now to truly succeed with their investments. With innovation, you need to have patience. It's a bit about timing. There's often cultural change that comes with it for organizations, especially big ones. The other big goal is to keep developing the platform and the methodology. We're going for an investment round in the US this year to really be able to go out there and hire the right people in different parts of the world to help more organizations succeed with innovation.

So you're really looking to be a global company.

We have one headquarters here and one in New York, and in addition to this, one part of the Innovation 360 business model is that we train licensed practitioners all over the world in using our platforms and methodology. We have about 200 licensed practitioners in twenty-eight countries, so we have different hubs around the world that are formed by wherever we have a high density of active practitioners. We're already in Asia, the Gulf, the EU, South America, Africa and the US. That's another way we plan to grow and scale up globally without having to hire too many people – really building on the magic and power of the gig economy.

But it all started in Stockholm. What was it about this city specifically?

Most of the founding members are from Stockholm. And, like myself, they've been out around in the world and then landed here again. So a lot of it is about bringing the right people together in the right place at the right time.

If I had a startup, why would I want to move here?

Well, we have fantastic weather. Just kidding. No, I think it's the social aspect. We have a social system, and events are often free and open. You don't have to get behind closed doors. You can literally build yourself a network in a really collaborative environment. There are also a lot of interesting areas of expertise in Stockholm, with universities supporting various initiatives by having different innovation hubs focusing on different industries. It's a beautiful city with good living standards, but it's quite expensive.

What advice would you give anyone looking to start a company in general?

I would give the same advice I give to all our customers, which is to ask, why are you doing this? What is the goal? Because often they get carried away by an idea but they haven't taken a step back and really thought about why they're doing this and for who. And is that 'who' even interested? Some people fall in love with a startup dream that seems very glamorous, but we have to remember that most startups never survive their one-year birthday; and if they do, they don't survive their second year birthday. It's very competitive.

What's the biggest mistake you've made?

We make mistakes all the time, but we see them as learning. I think it's important to make the mistakes as early as possible. What we could've done earlier is to decide what to focus on: whether we wanted to focus on the enterprise offering of our business or the subscription-based online business, we probably could have gone to market quicker, in a more crystal-clear way, if we'd picked one of those two paths earlier.

Okay, last question: why do you have so many hats?

I often get this question. It's actually by coincidence. One of my friends introduced me to her friend who'd started a hat company called BySju. She was this young entrepreneur from Slovenia living in London who quit her job to start a hat company. So I bought two hats from her because I wanted to support her, and also they were really good looking. Now I have nine hats, and I try to match them with the company brand I'm working with. If I work with a company that has a blue logo or I'm attending an event that has a blue logo, then I'll wear my blue hat to support them.

So you've got a hat for every occasion?

Exactly. And it fits perfectly because I can also switch roles very quickly. It becomes a fun metaphor. As a founder, you need to wear many hats, and you often have to switch several times during the day.

[About]   ideation360 develops methodologies and tools for organizations to manage their innovation initiatives. From data-driven analysis of strengths and capabilities to designing actionable change programs, ideation360 supports organizations that want to "walk the walk" when it comes to innovation.

[Links]   Web: **ideation360.com** Facebook: **ideation360x** Twitter: **@ideation360** Instagram: **ideation360**

What are your top work essentials?
Energy! My team! Our customers!

At what age did you found your company?
Twenty-seven.

What app do you use the most?
Email.

**What's the most valuable piece of advice
you've been given?**
Be the change you want to see in the world.

What's your greatest skill?
To wear many hats.

directory

Startups

Airinum AB
Östermalmsgatan 26A
11426 Stockholm
airinum.com

Amuse
Sankt Eriksgatan 63B
112 34 Stockholm
amuse.io

Gleechi
Maria Skolgata 83
Stockholm 11853
gleechi.com

Hi Henry
Regeringsgatan 65
113 53 Stockholm
hihenry.com

Mentimeter
Mariatorget 1 A
118 48 Stockholm
mentimeter.com

NuvoAir
Riddargatan 17D
114 57 Stockholm
nuvoair.com

Stilla
SUP46, Stockholm
Regeringsgatan 65
3rd floor
111 56 Stockholm
wearestilla.com

United Invitations
Birger Jarlsgatan 57C
113 56 Stockholm, Sweden
unitedinvitations.org

Watty
Sankt Göransgatan 159
Stockholm, Sweden, 11217
watty.io

Worldfavor AB
Munkbron 11,
111 28 Stockholm
worldfavor.com

Programs

Amplify Sweden
Valhallavägen 105
115 51 Stockholm

Ericsson AB
Torshamnsgatan 21
164 40 Kista, Sweden
ericsson.com

Founder Institute
Luntmakargatan 25
111 37 Stockholm
fi.co/home

Hyper Island
Telefonvägen 30
126 26 Hägersten
hyperisland.com

Ignite Sweden
C/O THINGS
Drottning Kristinas väg 53
114 28 Stockholm
ignitesweden.org

KTH Innovation
Lindstedtsvägen 24, 4th Floor
KTH Campus Valhallavägen
114 28 Stockholm
kth.se/innovation

SSES Ventures
Saltmätargatan 9
113 59 Stockholm
sses.se/ventures

Sting
KTH Campus Valhallavägen
Drottning Kristinas väg 53
114 28 Stockholm
sting.co/en

Sweden Foodtech Center Söderhallarna,
Medborgarplatsen 3
118 72 Stockholm
foodtechvillage.com

Spaces

A house
Östermalmsgatan 26A
114 26 Stockholm
ahousestockholm.com

Alma
Nybrogatan 8
114 34 Stockholm
thisisalma.com

Goto 10
Hammarby Kaj 10D
120 07 Stockholm
goto10.se

H2 Health Hub
Hälsingegatan 45
113 31 Stockholm
h2healthhub.com

Impact Hub Stockholm
Luntmakargatan 25
111 37, Stockholm
impacthub.se

Norrsken House
Birger Jarlsgatan 57C
113 56 Stockholm
norrskenhouse.org

Openlab
Valhallavägen 79
11428 Stockholm
openlabsthlm.se

The Park
Hälsingegatan 49
113 31 Stockholm
thepark.se

STHLM Music City
The Royal College of Music
Valhallavägen 105
11551 Stockholm

SUP46 - Startup People of Sweden
Regeringsgatan 65, 3F
11156 Stockholm
sup46.com

Experts

Business Sweden
World Trade Center
Klarabergsviadukten 70
111 64 Stockholm
business-sweden.se

Daimler AG
Corporate Headquarters
Mercedesstr. 137
70327 Stuttgart
Germany
daimler.com

Danske Bank Sverige
Norrmalmstorg 1
103 92 Stockholm
danskebank.se

EQT Partners AB
Blasieholmsgatan 3
111 48 Stockholm
Sweden
eqtpartners.com

SAS - Scandinavian Airlines
Frösundaviks Allé 1
169 70 Solna, Stockholm
flysas.com/en

Founders

ideation360
Olof Palmes gata 13
111 37 Stockholm
ideation360.com

Karma (Karmalicious AB)
Sankt Eriksgatan 63b
112 34 Stockholm
karma.life

Kidnovation
Sveavägen 44,
11134 Stockholm
kidnovation.se

Sana Labs
Nybrogatan 8
114 34 Stockholm
sanalabs.com

Zaver
Engelbrektsgatan 5,
114 32 Stockholm
zaver.se

Accountants

Grant Thornton
Sveavägen 20
103 94 Stockholm
grantthornton.se/en

PE accounting
Torsgatan 2, 2tr
111 23 Stockholm
accounting.pe

PwC
Torsgatan 21
113 97 Stockholm
pwc.com

Banks

Danske Bank
danskebank.se

Handelsbanken
handelsbanken.se/sv

Nordea
nordea.se

SEB
seb.se

Swedbank
swedbank.se

Coffee Shops and Places with Wifi

Café & Co
cafeco.se/en

Coffice
coffice.coop/en

Drop Café
dropcoffee.com/pages/
the-cafe

Il Caffe
ilcaffe.se

Johan & Nyström
johanochnystrom.se

Startup Café by Sup46
sup46.com/startupcafe

Flats and Rentals

Andrahand
andrahand.se

Blocket
blocket.se

Bostaddirekt
bostaddirekt.com

Bostadsförmedlingen
bostad.stockholm.se/english

Collective living:K9 Co-living / Hus 24
techfarm.life/hus24
k9coliving.com/about/

Hyrabostad
hyrabostad.se

Qasa
en.qasa.se

Facebook Groups:
Bostad Stockholm
Bostadstockholm
Bostäder Stockholm
Lägenhet i Stockholm
Lägenheter i Stockholm

Expat Groups and Meetups

Expats in Sweden
facebook.com/groups/
expatsinsweden

Expat World Sthlm
facebook.com/groups/
expatsclubstockholm

Grow international
growinternationals.com

Internations
internations.org

Stockholm AI
stockholm.ai

Stockholm entrepreneurs
stockholmentrepreneurs.se

Startup Grind
startupgrind.com

Stockholm tech meetup
meetup.com/en-AU/
STHLM-Tech-Meetup

Silicon Vikings
siliconvikings.com

Important Government Offices

Almi
almi.se/en/in-english

Business Sweden
business-sweden.se

Försäkringskassan (Swedish social insurance Agency)
forsakringskassan.se

IFS (the International Entrepreneurs Association in Sweden)
ifs.a.se/home

Migrationsverket (Swedish migration agency)
migrationsverket.se

NyföretagarCentrum
nyforetagarcentrum.com/
in-english/

Skatteverket (Swedish tax agency)
skatteverket.se

Stockholm Chamber of Commerce
chamber.se/

Tillväxtverket (Swedish agency for economic and regional growth)
tillvaxtverket.se

Incubators and Accelerators

KI science park
kisciencepark.se/en

500
500.co

Insurance Companies

Folksam
folksam.se

IF
if.se

Trygghansa
trygghansa.se

Language Schools

Folkuniversitet
folkuniversitetet.se

Medborgarskolan
medborgarskolan.se

Online
learningswedish.se/courses/11

Sensus
sensus.se

SFI
stockholm.se/sfi

SIFA
sifa.stockholm.se

Investors

Almi invest
almi.se/Almi-Invest

Atomico
atomico.com

Bonnier ventures
bonnierventures.com

Creandum
creandum.com

EQT ventures
eqtventures.com

Industrifonden
industrifonden.com

Luminar ventures
luminarventures.com

Moor
moorcap.com

Northzone
northzone.com

Serendipity Innovation
serendipity.se

Startup Events

Femtech
sup46.com/event/femtech-11-
created-for-women-by-women

me Convention
me-convention.com

Sting Day
stingday.se

Stockholm tech fest
sthlm-tech-fest-2017.confetti.
events

Sweden foodtech
swedenfoodtech.com

Symposium
brilliantminds.symposium.co

Start up Gala
sup46.com/events/swedish-
startup-hall-fame

Venture Cup
venturecup.se

glossary

A

Accelerator
An organization or program that offers advice and resources to help small businesses grow

Acqui-hire
Buying out a company based on the skills of its staff rather than its service or product

Angel Investment
Outside funding with shared ownership equity

API
Application programming interface

ARR
Accounting (or average) rate of return: calculation generated from net income of the proposed capital investment

Artificial Intelligence
The simulation of human intelligence by computer systems; machines that are able to perform tasks normally carried out by humans

B

B2B
(Business-to-Business)
The exchange of services, information and/or products from a business to a business

B2C
(Business-to-Consumer)
The exchange of services, information and/or products from a business to a consumer

Blockchain
A digital and public collection of financial accounts for all cryptocurrency transactions

BOM
(Bill of Materials)
A list of the parts or components required to build a product

Bootstrap
To self-fund, without outside investment

Bridge Loan
A loan taken out for a short-term period, typically between two weeks and three years, until long-term financing can be organized

Burn Rate
The amount of money a startup spends

Business Angel
An experienced entrepreneur or professional who provides starting or growth capital for promising startups

Business Model Canvas
A template that gives a coherent overview of the key drivers of a business in order to bring innovation into current or new business models

C

C-level
Chief position

Cap Table
An analysis of ownership stakes in a company

CMO
Chief marketing officer

Cold-Calling
The solicitation of potential customers who had no prior interaction with the solicitor

Convertible Note/Loan
A type of short-term debt often used by seed investors to delay establishing a valuation for the startup until a later round of funding or milestone

Coworking
A shared working environment

CPA
Cost per action

CPC
Cost per click

Cybersecurity
Technologies, processes and practices designed to protect against the criminal or unauthorized use of electronic data

D

Dealflow
Term for investors that refers to the rate at which they receive potential business deals

Deeptech
Companies founded on the discoveries or innovations of technologists and scientists

Diluting
A reduction in the ownership percentage of a share of stock due to new equity shares being issued

E

Elevator Pitch
A short summary used to quickly define a product or idea

Ethereum
A blockchain-based software platform and programming language that helps developers build and publish distributed applications

Exit
A way to transition the ownership of a company to another company

F

Fintech
Financial technology

Flex Desk
Shared desk in a space where coworkers are free to move around and sit wherever they like

I

Incubator
Facility established to nurture young startup firms during their first few months or years of development

Installed Base
The number of units of a certain type of product that have been sold and are actually being used

IP
(Intellectual Property) Property which is not tangible; the result of creativity, such as patents and copyrights

IPO
(Initial Public Offering) The first time a company's stock is offered for sale to the public

K

KPI
(Key Performance Indicator)
A value that is measurable and demonstrates how effectively a company is achieving key business objectives

L

Later-Stage
More mature startups/companies

Lean
Refers to 'lean startup methodology;' the method proposed by Eric Ries in his book for developing businesses and startups through product development cycles

Lean LaunchPad
A methodology for entrepreneurs to test and develop business models based on inquiring with and learning from customers

M

M&A
(Mergers and Acquisitions) A merger is when two companies join to form a new company, while an acquisition is the purchase of one company by another where no new company is formed

MAU
Monthly active users

MVP
Minimum viable product

O

Opportunities Fund
Investment in companies or sectors in areas where growth opportunities are anticipated

P

P2P
(Peer-to-Peer)
A network created when two or more PCs are connected and sharing resources without going through a separate server

Pitch Deck
A short version of a business plan presenting key figures generally to investors

PR Kit (Press Kit)
Package of promotional materials, such as pictures, logos and descriptions of a company

Product-Market Fit
When a product has created significant customer value and its best target industries have been identified

Pro-market
A market economy/a capitalistic economy

S

SaaS
Software as a service

Scaleup
A company that has already validated its product in a market and is economically sustainable

Seed Funding
First round, small, early-stage investment from family members, friends, banks or an investor

Seed Investor
An investor focusing on the seed round

Seed Round
The first round of funding

Series A/B/C/D
The name of funding rounds that come after the seed stage

Shares
Units of ownership of a company that belong to a shareholder

Solopreneurs
A person who sets up and runs a business on their own and typically does not hire employees

Startup
Companies under three years old, in the growth stage and becoming profitable (if not already)

SVP
Senior Vice President

T

Term Sheet/Letter of Intent
The document between an investor and a startup including the conditions for financing (commonly non-binding)

U

Unicorn
A company often in the tech or software sector worth over US$1 billion

USP
Unique selling point

UX
(User experience design) The process of designing and improving user satisfaction with products so that they are useful, easy to use and pleasurable to interact with

V

VC
(Venture Capital) Financing from a pool of investors in a venture capital firm in return for equity

Vesting
Process that involves giving or earning a right to a present or future payment, benefit or asset

Z

Zebras
Companies which aim for sustainable prosperity and are powered by people who work together to create change beyond a positive financial return

STARTUP GUIDE TRONDHEIM — The Entrepreneur's Handbook
STARTUP GUIDE HAMBURG — The Entrepreneur's Handbook
STARTUP GUIDE LUXEMBOURG — The Entrepreneur's Handbook
STARTUP GUIDE VIENNA — The Entrepreneur's Handbook
STARTUP GUIDE TEL AVIV — The Entrepreneur's Handbook
STARTUP GUIDE MADRID — The Entrepreneur's Handbook
STARTUP GUIDE VALENCIA — The Entrepreneur's Handbook
STARTUP GUIDE COPENHAGEN — The Entrepreneur's Handbook
STARTUP GUIDE PARIS — The Entrepreneur's Handbook
STARTUP GUIDE REYKJAVIK — The Entrepreneur's Handbook
STARTUP GUIDE STOCKHOLM — The Entrepreneur's Handbook
STARTUP GUIDE MUNICH — The Entrepreneur's Handbook
STARTUP GUIDE FRANKFURT — The Entrepreneur's Handbook
STARTUP GUIDE ZURICH — The Entrepreneur's Handbook
STARTUP GUIDE LONDON — The Entrepreneur's Handbook
STARTUP GUIDE LISBON — The Entrepreneur's Handbook
STARTUP GUIDE NEW YORK — The Entrepreneur's Handbook
STARTUP GUIDE BERLIN — The Entrepreneur's Handbook
STARTUP GUIDE OSLO — The Entrepreneur's Handbook

→ startupguide.com   Follow us

About the Guide

Based on traditional guidebooks that can be carried around everywhere, Startup Guide books help you navigate and connect with different startup scenes across the globe. Each book is packed with useful information, exciting entrepreneur stories and insightful interviews with local experts. We hope the book will become your trusted companion as you embark on a new (startup) journey. Today, Startup Guide books are in seventeen different cities in Europe, the US and the Middle East, including Berlin, London, New York, Tel Aviv, Stockholm, Copenhagen, Vienna, Lisbon and Paris.

How we make the guides:

To ensure an accurate and trustworthy guide every time, we team up with a city partner that is established in the local startup scene. We then ask the local community to nominate startups, coworking spaces, founders, schools, investors, incubators and established businesses to be featured through an online submission form. Based on the results, these submissions are narrowed down to the top hundred organizations and individuals. Next, the local advisory board – which is selected by our community partner and consists of key players in the local startup community – votes for the final selection, ensuring a balanced representation of industries and startup stories in each book. The local community partner then works in close collaboration with our international editorial and design team to help research, organize interviews with journalists as well as plan photoshoots with photographers. Finally, all content is reviewed, edited and put into the book's layout by the Startup Guide team in Berlin and Lisbon before going for print in Berlin.

Where to find us: The easiest way to get your hands on a Startup Guide book is to order it from our online shop: startupguide.com/books

If you prefer to do things in real life, drop by one of the fine retailers listed on the stockists page on our website.

Want to become a stockist or suggest a store?

Get in touch here: sales@startupguide.com

STARTUP
GUIDE
STORE

The Startup Guide Stores

Whether it's sniffing freshly printed books
or holding an innovative product, we're huge fans of
physical experiences. That's why we opened two
stores – one in Lisbon and another in Berlin.
Not only do the stores showcase our books
and curated products, they're also our offices
and a place for the community to come together
to share wows and hows. Say hello!

Lisbon:

R. Rodrigues de Faria 103
Edifício G6, 1300 - 501 Lisboa
Tue-Sun: 12h-19h
+351 21 139 8791
lisbon@startupguide.com

Berlin:

Waldemarstraße 38, 10999 Berlin
Mon-Fri: 10h-18h
+49 (0)30-37468679
berlin@startupguide.com

#startupeverywhere

Startup Guide is a creative content and publishing company founded by Sissel Hansen in 2014.
We produce guidebooks and tools to help entrepreneurs navigate and connect with different startup
scenes across the globe. As the world of work changes, our mission is to guide, empower and inspire
people to start their own business anywhere. Today, Startup Guide books are in 17 different cities
in Europe, the US and the Middle East, including Berlin, London, Tel Aviv, Stockholm, Copenhagen,
Vienna, Lisbon and Paris. We also have two physical stores in Berlin and Lisbon to promote and sell
products by startups. Startup Guide is a 20-person team based in Berlin and Lisbon.
Visit our site for more: startupguide.com

Want to get more info, be a partner or say hello?

Shoot us an email here info@startupguide.com

Join us and #startupeverywhere

Stockholm Advisory Board

Jonas Almeling
Head of Innovation & Ecosystem
Business Sweden

Oskar Malm Wiklund
Member Experience & Tech
Norrsken Foundation

Sonia Kaurah
Community Manager
SUP46

Birk Jernström
General Manager &
Co-founder
Tictail

Anne Lidgard
Director, Silicon
Valley Office
Vinnova

Tetiana Siianko
Program Manager
Sweden Foodtech /
Techstars Startup Weekend

Julia Selander
CEO
Venture Cup Sweden

Jenny Theolin
Designer & Educator
Studio Theolin

Neil S W Murray
Founding Partner
The Nordic Web

Joseph Michael
CMO
TVM

With thanks to our **Content Partners**

And our **Community Partner**

me Convention
/ FRONT ROW TICKETS
TO THE FUTURE

The start of inspiring ideas

The me Convention, a unique conference and festival event, aims to connect bright minds across all industries in order to shape the future. The first me Convention, a collaboration between Mercedes-Benz and SXSW, was held in 2017 in Frankfurt, Germany. As proven leaders in innovation and leadership, both brands bring together global experts and pioneers across art, music, technology, science and more to inspire unique conversations and the exchange of knowledge.

Top speakers at the first event included Facebook COO Sheryl Sandberg, astronaut and space explorer Buzz Aldrin, avant-garde artist and the world's first cyborg Neil Harbisson, sociologist Auma Obama, art curator Hans-Ulrich Obrist, IBM Fellow John Cohn, and fashion icon Amber Valletta. Following the huge success of the platform, the me Convention experience was brought to SXSW in 2018 by cohosting SXSW's Intelligent Future Track at Fairmont Hotel, offering extraordinary talks from forward-thinking leaders and presenting engaging activities in a festival-like setup in iconic Palm Park.

Hej, me Convention Stockholm

After premiering in Frankfurt and hot off the heels of Austin, the me Convention will next be held in Stockholm. Explore the entrepreneurial spirit of Sweden's vibrant capital and join today's makers and thought leaders for the me Convention 2018 at Nacka Strandsmässan. Pioneers from all industries will come together for cutting-edge conversations and to reveal some of tomorrow's most innovative technologies. Join us and explore our 2018 themes – New Society, New Leadership, New Economies, New Creativity, and New Bionomics – plus experience an outstanding evening program including concerts, art exhibitions, parties and film screenings.

The future is unwritten, so bring your pens to #createthenew.

[Links]   Web: me-convention.com Facebook: meconvention Twitter: @meconvention

WHERE NEXT?